Becoming an

EZER

Guided Journal for Women

A 12-Week Journey into God's Design

for Strength, Purpose, and Partnership

Karen Rich

Skinny Brown Dog Media

Dedication

To my mother, Bettie Perkins-Mosley, and to every woman who has ever been told she was "just" anything—a role, a title, a helper, or less than. HEAR THIS! You are a force of strength, a well of wisdom, and a source of great influence. You were designed to stand on the level playing field of the brave, to bring light to a dark world, and to be a catalyst for change wherever you go. This journal is your training ground. COME! Sharpen and discover your voice, strengthen your spirit, and step boldly into the purpose-driven call you were designed for. The world needs all of who you are.

Author Bio

My name is Karen Rich, and I am the founder of Reap Her Ministries. For more than 18 years, I had the honor of serving as a missionary with Youth With A Mission (YWAM), with much of my ministry taking place throughout South America—particularly Argentina, Chile, and Ecuador. Those years deeply shaped my faith, my calling, and my passion for helping women understand who they are through God's eyes.

Through discipleship, teaching, and walking closely with women from many different backgrounds, I have witnessed how powerfully lives— including my own—are transformed when women grasp their true identity in Christ. Although I am still on this journey of understanding myself, I long to see women rooted in biblical truth, healed by God's love, and empowered by the Holy Spirit to live boldly in their God-given purpose. Much of my teaching centers on God's original design for women, including the rich biblical meaning of Ezer—a word that reveals strength, partnership, and divine purpose. This is a lifelong journey.

I am married to my husband, Charles Rich. Together we have raised six wonderful children: Brianna Lattuada and Joseph Lattuada, Justin Rich, Jessica Borland, Jared Rich, and Jacob Rich. Faith, family, and community are central to my life and ministry, continually reminding me that faith is meant to be lived out with love, humility, and joy.

Reap Her was born out of a divinely appointed moment when Charles sent me a short video clip that became the catalyst for this journal and a turning point in my own journey to becoming an Ezer. Through the Scripture, prayer, and application of the teachings found here, it is my desire that this journal will be a sacred space for you to encounter God, rediscover your worth, and step confidently into the calling He has placed on your life.

You are seen. You are valued. You are *Ezer.*

How to Get the Most from This Guided Journal

This guided journal is meant to walk with you over the next thirteen weeks. It is not a test to pass or a race to finish. Give yourself permission to slow down, listen for God's voice, and let truth settle deeply in your heart.

Choose a Daily Time with God
Set aside 15–20 minutes each day when you can be as uninterrupted as possible. Morning, lunchtime, or evening—whatever works best for you. Bring your Bible, this journal, and a pen.

Follow the Daily Flow

Each day includes four parts. Move through them in order:

Scripture – Read the passage slowly, more than once if you can. Ask the Holy Spirit to highlight a word or phrase that stands out to you.

Insight – This short teaching helps connect the Scripture to what it means to live as an Ezer—strong, called, and partnered with God. Let it invite you to see God and yourself in a fresh way.

Reflection – Use the questions to talk honestly with God. Write your thoughts, prayers, or even one sentence that captures what is stirring in you. There are no "right" answers—only honest ones.

Application – Here you will be invited to take one small step in response to what you've read. Ask, "What is one thing I can do today or this week?" and write it down.

Honor Day Seven
Each week closes with a seventh day set aside for review and prayer. Look back over your notes:

What theme, verse, or insight stayed with you?

Where did you sense God's presence?

What did you notice about yourself—your thoughts, feelings, or patterns?

Use this space to thank God, confess where you struggled, and ask for renewed strength.

Give Yourself Grace
If you miss a day—or even several—do not start over. Simply begin again on the next unfinished page. This is a journey of becoming, not perfection. God is far more interested in your heart than in a perfectly completed journal.

As you move through these pages, expect God to meet you. He has always called you Ezer. This is your time to discover what that means and to walk it out, one day at a time.

Acknowledgments

To my mother, Bettie Perkins-Mosley, my bonus moms, Jackie Sheppard, Edna Brunelle-McGraw, Martha Rodriguez, Rosana Liste, Suzanne Housewright-Cook and my sister-in-love, Debbie Perkins, thank you for lovingly and valiantly teaching me the innate strength and importance of embracing my femininity as God designed.

To my late daddy, Paul Perkins Sr., in the all-too-short length of time you were with us, you taught me so much. First, you led me into my walk with Jesus as Savior and were pivotal in helping me understand God's call on my life to missions. As it relates to this body of work, you taught me that just because I was a girl never meant that I was any less than the boys. That I was different, yes, but just as capable and called as anyone else. Unknowingly, you were laying the foundations of my own journey to becoming an Ezer.

To my brother, Paul Perkins Jr., thank you for always being there for me and loving me, even when you did not always understand where—or to what—I was headed.

To my late husband, Jorge Lattuada, thank you for choosing me to be your wife for thirteen years and for showing me that I was worthy of godly human love. Thank you for being a good father to our children, Brianna and Joseph. Thank you, even in your absence, for helping me discover that I am stronger than I ever imagined I could be.

To my main peeps, my daughter and son, Brianna and Joseph Lattuada. Thank you for loving me even in the many moments that I was anything but loveable. Thank you for giving me the courage to move forward in the less than ideal circumstances that this lifes journey has taken us. Thank you for cheering me on when I felt like giving up. Thank you for making me a better mama, woman and friend. Most of all, thank you for, in your own unique ways, bringing me closer to God. You are loved more than you will ever know.

To every woman over the years who allowed me the privilege of sharing God's love, redemption, and healing in my own life to encourage and uplift them in their journeys, thank you for allowing me that space.

To my husband, Charles Rich, I am ever indebted to you for getting this project started with the simple act of sending a video clip. You encourage me in my place as your helper and tell me that I was—and am—doing a good job every day. Although you had no idea of its impact, that one act will hopefully reach millions of women around the world through this journal.

Lastly, yet foremost, to God my Father: You called me Ezer long before I was born. You designed me and all women to help others in ways they cannot help themselves. Just as You delivered Your chosen people of Israel from captivity, may You work through me and this journal to help women all over the world walk out of the darkness of being "less than" into the light of the powerful role You designed us for. May this gift be exponentially multiplied to others.

Month 1: God's Intent for Ezer

Our focus is on the meaning of Ezer and how it reflects God's design for woman. We will explore how, as a reflection of God's LOVE, this design reflects inherent strength and purpose allowing us to practically build and strengthen one another in community.

Week 1: God's Design for Ezer

To understand the original intent of Ezer as a reflection of God's strength, purpose, and partnership.

Day 1: Helper (Ezer)

Date: _________________________

Genesis 2:18: "Then the Lord God said, 'It is not good for the man to be alone. I will make a HELPER who is JUST RIGHT for him.'"

INSIGHT

Growing up in the rural South, being called a "helper" wasn't exactly an esteemed title. It conjured images of someone relegated to the background, useful but not essential... The Hebrew term Ezer shatters these cultural misconceptions entirely. It describes a strong and essential helper - one who exemplifies power rather than passivity. An Ezer doesn't complete what is lacking by becoming less. She fulfills God's design for women bringing completion as she walks in her full strength, wisdom, perspective, and capabilities.

REFLECTION

How does the word Ezer change the way you view God's purpose for your life?

____

____

____

____

____

____

APPLICATION

Journal how you can live out your role as a strong helper in your relationships and community.

____

____

____

____

____

Date: ________________

Psalm 33:20: "We put our hope in the Lord. He is our HELP and our shield."

INSIGHT

In this passage, the same word Ezer is used to describe God. We would never think of God being less than anyone or anything. His help is essential to our very existence, helping us in ways that we simply cannot help ourselves. As a reflection of the Living God, we can demonstrate that being a helper comes from a place of power and protection.

REFLECTION

How does understanding God as your helper encourage you to reflect His strength?

____

____

____

____

____

____

APPLICATION

Identify an area where you need God's strength today and write a prayer asking for His help.

____

____

____

____

____

Day 3: Partnership

Date: _______________________

Ecclesiastes 4:9-12: "Two people are better off than one, for they can help each other succeed. If one person falls, the other can reach out and help. But someone who falls alone is in real trouble. Likewise, two people lying close together can keep each other warm. But how can one be warm alone? A person standing alone can be attacked and defeated, but two can stand back-to-back and conquer. Three are even better, for a triple-braided cord is not easily broken."

INSIGHT

In our culture, there is an unfair expectation on women that we be able to do anything and everything a man can do. But God's design for relationships, is that we be complimentary to one another, reflecting His relational nature. I have heard it said that in any relationship, if we are both exactly the same, bringing the same strengths and talents to the table, then one of us in that relationship isn't necessary. An Ezer strengthens and uplifts those she works along side of.

REFLECTION

How can you be an effective partner in your relationships, reflecting God's design?

____

____

____

____

____

____

APPLICATION

Commit to one action today that supports someone in your life, whether through encouragement, service, or prayer. Write it down, and then DO IT!

____

____

____

Day 4: Purpose

Date: ________________

Jeremiah 29:11: "'For I know the plans I have for you,' says the Lord. 'They are plans for good and not for disaster, to give you a future and a hope.'"

INSIGHT

Although this is my life verse, I confess that I have not always walked very well in its promise. When life gets hard, it is easy to forget that God created you and I with a specific purpose in mind, uniquely equipping us to fulfill our roles in His plan.

REFLECTION

How does understanding God's purpose for you give you confidence?

____

____

____

____

____

____

APPLICATION

Write down one area where you feel called to grow or serve and ask God for clarity and boldness to step into it.

____

____

____

____

____

Day 5: Reflection of God

Date: _____________________

Psalm 139:13-14: "You made all the delicate, inner parts of my body and knit me together in my mother's womb. Thank you for making me so wonderfully complex! Your workmanship is marvelous - how well I know

INSIGHT

God took great care in creating each of us, men and women alike. We are not less than... we are complementary to... As a reflection of God's image, we are fearfully and wonderfully made, uniquely designed to display His attributes to the world.

REFLECTION

In what ways do you see God's image reflected in yourself?

____

____

____

____

____

____

APPLICATION

Write Psalm 139:14 in your journal and personalize it as a prayer, affirming your identity in Christ.

____

____

____

____

____

Day 6: Unique Role

Date: ___________________

1 Corinthians 12:4-7: "There are different kinds of spiritual gifts, but the same Spirit is the source of them all. There are different kinds of service, but we serve the same Lord. God works in different ways, but it is the same God who does the work in all of us. A spiritual gift is given to each of us so we can help each other."

INSIGHT

Each person has unique spiritual gifts to use for God's glory. Your gifts and my gifts are an integral part of the body of Christ.

REFLECTION

What specific gifts has God given you? How are you using them?

____

____

____

____

____

____

____

APPLICATION

Use one of your spiritual gifts to serve others today, whether through encouragement, teaching, or acts of service. Write down how God used you today.

____

____

____

____

____

Date: _______________

REFLECTION

Review the week's insights on Ezer. How has your understanding of God's design for you changed?

____

____

____

____

____

PRAYER

Write a prayer of thanksgiving for the ways God has revealed His purpose and strength through your identity as an Ezer.

____

____

____

____

____

____

Week 2: Ezer as Strength

To explore how the strength of Ezer reflects God's nature and EMPOWERS women to fulfill His mission.

Day 1: Warrior

Date: ________________

Deuteronomy 33:29: "How blessed are you O Israel! Who else is like you, a people saved by the Lord? HE is your protecting shield and your triumphant sword! Your enemies will cringe before YOU, and YOU WILL STOMP ON THEIR BACKS!"

INSIGHT

After my first husband passed away, it felt like I was left a young widow with two children to raise... alone. I was grieving his loss, not only for myself, but for our children as well. We were homeless and had no source of income. I was terrified and overwhelmed with the life that lay before me without my husband. Over time, God showed himself a faithful husband and father. Here, God is described as a shield and helper, equipping His people for battle. With his help, both of the kids are grown and are living their own lives. God provided a home through Habitat for Humanity, and we have never gone without anything that we needed. As an Ezer, you embody the strength to face life's challenges with His help.

REFLECTION

What battles in your life require God's strength?

____

____

____

____

____

____

APPLICATION

Write a prayer surrendering one specific challenge to God and asking for His help.

____

____

____

Day 2: Refuge

Date: _______________________

Psalm 46:1: "GOD is our refuge and our strength, ALWAYS ready to help in times of trouble."

INSIGHT

Honestly, I can't imagine how folks do life without God being the central part of their lives. Who do they run to in difficult times? In what or where do they find the answers they so desperately need? I know of only one whom I can run to. Once I led an outreach team with my late husband to the Ecuadorian Amazon Jungle. We were dropped in the middle of nowhere where we were to catch another bus to our final destination. Apparently, the driver did not get the message as he passed us by, not even slowing down. There we were with eight students looking to us for answers of how to resolve this quandary we found ourselves in. The next morning, we were informed by the locals that there would not be another form of transport to our destination for another week! So, we prayed that God send HELP!! Five minutes later, off in the distance, we saw a cloud of dust and heard the rumble of an engine. To our amazement, the village we were headed to had placed an additional order for provisions that week. Their request for now became our provision and the answer to our prayerful need. We all climbed aboard and got to where we needed to be. God showed up as our EZER and did for us what we were unable to do for ourselves. God is our refuge and strength, an ever-present help in times of trouble. As an Ezer, YOU reflect this strength by offering support and refuge to others.

REFLECTION

Where do you go for refuge in difficult times?

____

____

____

____

____

____

____

APPLICATION

Identify someone in your life who needs encouragement and offer them a word of support or prayer today. Write down their name and what your impartation to them.

____

____

____

____

____

____

____

Day 3: Protector

Date: ________________

Exodus 18:4: "His second son was named EliEzer, for Moses had said, 'The God of my ancestors was my HELPER; he rescued me from the sword of Pharaoh.'"

INSIGHT

Moses named his son EliEzer, meaning "My God is my help," in honor of God's protection during trials. I am so thankful that we can call on God to help us. Perhaps along with saying "Praise the Lord" in challenging times, we all should shout out "ELIEZER" as well. Personally, I need a daily reminder that God is my helper. Don't we all?

REFLECTION

How has God protected you in your life?

____

____

____

____

____

____

APPLICATION

Share a story with someone about how God has been your protector.

____

____

____

____

Day 4: Boldness

Date: _________________

Judges 4:4-9: "Deborah, the wife of Lapidoth, was a prophet who was judging Israel at that time. She would sit under the Palm of Deborah, between Ramah and Bethel in the hill country of Ephraim, and the Israelites would go to her for judgment. One day she sent for Barak son of Abinoam, who lived in Kedesh in the land of Naphtali. She said to him, 'This is what the Lord, the God of Israel, commands you: Call out 10,000 warriors from the tribes of Naphtali and Zebulun at Mount Tabor. And I will call out Sisera, commander of Jabin's army, along with his chariots and warriors, to the Kishon River. There I will give you victory over him.' Barak told her, 'I will go, but only if YOU go with me.' 'Very well,' she said. 'I will go with you. But you will receive no honor in this venture, for the Lord's victory over Sisera will be at the hands of a woman.' So, Deborah went with Barak to Kadesh."

INSIGHT

Sometimes, in fact most times, stepping out into an area that is unfamiliar to us can be downright scary. Even when we are certain that it is God himself who is asking us to step out into a vision, and if we are honest, we are no different than Barak. Deborah's boldness as a judge and leader exemplifies the strength of an Ezer. We are like Deborah when we choose to step out in faith and boldness.

REFLECTION

Where is God calling you to act with boldness and faith?

____

____

____

____

____

____

____

APPLICATION

Take one bold step today in an area where you've been hesitant to act, trusting God to guide you. Record here What God had you do.

Day 5: Sustainer

Date: _________________

Isaiah 41:10: "DON'T be afraid, for I am with you. DON'T be discouraged, for I AM your God. I WILL strengthen you and help you. I WILL hold you up with my victorious right hand."

INSIGHT

God strengthens and sustains His people, enabling them to sustain others. I have seen this in my own journey. Earlier this week I shared briefly about being unexpectedly faced with raising my children on my own. I did not ask to be a single parent. But God, in His love and grace, sustained us every step of the way. He gave us strength each day. And while we may not have had all the things we wanted, we never went a single day without having exactly what we needed. He calmed our fears, brought folks into our lives to encourage us. I can boldly say, God sustained us in every way.

REFLECTION

Who in your life needs your support today?

____

____

____

____

____

____

____

APPLICATION

Offer practical help or encouragement to someone in need, reflecting God's sustaining power. Who did you help, and in what way(s)?

____

____

____

Day 6: Strength in Weakness

Date: _____________________

2 Corinthians 12:9-10: "Each time he said, 'My grace is all you need. My power works best in weakness.' So now I am glad to boast about my weakness, so that the power of Christ can work through me. That's why I take pleasure in my weakness, and in the insults, hardships, persecutions, and troubles I suffer for Christ. For when I am weak, then I am strong."

INSIGHT

Have you ever wondered if Jesus had any "weak" areas? I mean, He was one hundred percent divine, but He was also one hundred percent man. God's power was on full display through Jesus' resurrection. When we lean into our weaknesses, God's power is made perfect, allowing His strength to shine through.

REFLECTION

How can embracing your weakness draw you closer to God and reflect His glory?

____

____

____

____

____

____

APPLICATION

Write a prayer asking God to use your weaknesses for His purposes.

____

____

____

____

Date: ________________

REFLECTION

Reflect on how God's strength has been evident in your life this week. How has it changed your view of being an Ezer?

____

____

____

____

____

____

PRAYER

Write a prayer of gratitude for the ways God empowers and strengthens you to fulfill His calling.

____

____

____

____

____

____

Week 3: Ezer in Relationships

To discover how Ezer reflects God's RELATIONAL nature and builds STRONG connections.

Day 1: Loyalty (Ruth)

Date: _______________________

Ruth 1:16-17: "But Ruth replied, 'Don't ask me to leave you and turn back. Wherever you go, I will go; wherever you live, I will live. Your people will be my people, and your God will be my God. Wherever you die, I will die, and there I will be buried. May the Lord punish me severely if I allow anything but death to separate us!'"

INSIGHT

Do you remember your best friend from high school? I do. In fact, she bears the name of Ruth's mother-in-law, Naomi. We did everything together, were always there for each other. We each even had a friendship necklace. Each of us had one half of a heart. It was our way of saying that we were a part of each other. Over the years we have had less and less contact, living our own lives, but that loyalty still remains. Ruth's loyalty to Naomi demonstrates the steadfast love and commitment of an Ezer. Her faithfulness paved the way for God's greater plan.

REFLECTION

Where in your relationships is God calling you to demonstrate steadfast loyalty?

____

____

____

____

____

____

APPLICATION

Identify one relationship where you can show loyalty today, whether through a phone call, encouragement, or an act of service.

____

____

____

Day 2: Redemption (Naomi and Ruth)

Date: ___________________

Ruth 4:13-17: "So Boaz took Ruth into his home, and she became his wife. When he slept with her, the Lord enabled her to become pregnant, and she gave birth to a son. Then the women of the town said to Naomi, 'Praise the Lord, who has now provided a redeemer for your family! May this child be famous in Israel. May he restore your youth and care for you in your old age. For he is the son of your daughter-in-law who loves you and has been better to you than seven sons!' Naomi took the baby and cuddled him to her breast. And she cared for him as if he were her own. The neighbor women Said, 'Now at last Naomi has a son again!' And they named him Obed. He became the father of Jesse and the grandfather of David."

INSIGHT

My husband Charles and I have known one another for over twenty-five years and married on September 15, 2024. My first Husband and I were in ministry together with Charles for several months before Jorge went to be with Jesus. I left ministry to mourn my great loss and raise my children. Charles and I had very limited contact for the next twelve years. In April of 2024, Charles put out an ad on Facebook for some help with some house cleaning that as a two-time stroke survivor, he was not able to do on his own. I answered the ad and as we were putting the carpet cleaner back in the car, he asked me on a date. Not only was our relationship redeemed, but also our mutual dreams of ministry together for the Kingdom. Naomi's restoration and Ruth's role in the lineage of Christ reveal how God redeems relationships and uses them for His purposes.

REFLECTION

In what ways has God brought redemption to your relationships?

____

____

____

____

____

____

____

APPLICATION

Reflect on a challenging relationship and ask God to redeem and restore it for His glory.

____

____

____

____

____

____

Date: _________________

1 Samuel 25:23-35: "When Abigail saw David, she quickly got off her donkey and bowed low before him. She fell at his feet and said, 'I accept all blame in this matter, my lord. Please listen to what I have to say. I know Nabal is a wicked and ill-tempered man; please don't pay any attention to him. He's a fool, just as his name suggests. But I never even saw the young men you sent. Now, my lord, surely as the Lord lives and you yourself live, since the Lord has kept you from murdering and taking vengeance into your own hands, let all your enemies and all those who try to harm you, be as cursed as Nabal is. And here is a present that I, your servant, have brought to you and your young men.'"

INSIGHT

An advocate stands in the gap between one person and another of usually higher authority in some way. As moms, we may do this for our child with authorities at school. As wives, we may advocate in prayer for our husbands when they are facing difficult situations. As friends, we may advocate for another who is walking through some sort of injustice in their personal lives. As a demonstration of faith in God's call to love and support others who are in need, part of being an Ezer is a call to advocacy. Abigail's wisdom and courage protected her household and honored God. As an Ezer, she acted as a mediator and advocate.

REFLECTION

Where in your life can you act as an advocate for peace or righteousness?

____

____

____

____

____

____

APPLICATION

Seek out an opportunity to advocate for someone today, whether through prayer, encouragement, or practical help. What did you do?

Day 4: Sacrifice

Date: _______________________

John 15:13: "There is no greater love than to lay down one's life for one's friends."

INSIGHT

There is so much that we could say about this one short verse. Jesus teaches that true love involves self-sacrifice. As an Ezer, you reflect God's love by putting others' needs before your own. If you are a mother, wife, or friend, loving your child, spouse or friend will always mean self-sacrifice in one way or another. For our kids it may mean going without something we want in order that they may have what they need. With your husband, it may be something as simple as sacrificing and episode of Friends that you have seen a million times, for Sunday night football. For a friend, it could be going out of your way to give them a ride to work because their car is in the shop. All of our sacrifices will be different, but those sacrifices will be necessary if we are to say that we truly love someone.

REFLECTION

How can you practice sacrificial love in your relationships?

____

____

____

____

____

____

APPLICATION

Choose one act of sacrificial love today, such as offering forgiveness, giving generously, or serving someone in need.

____

____

____

Day 5: Honoring Others

Date: _________________

Philippians 2:3-4: "Don't be selfish; don't try to impress others. Be humble, thinking of others as better than yourselves. Don't look out only for your own interests but take an interest in others too."

INSIGHT

Have you ever had one of those moments with your kids that you asked them to do something, and although they said that they would, they rolled their eyes as they went off to perform the delegated task. If you are a parent, the answer is a most definite and resounding YES! Did you feel honored, or respected, or like you mattered? I know I never have. And honestly, it has made my relationship with my kiddos very challenging at times. Relationships thrive when we honor and value others above ourselves. An Ezer models humility and selflessness.

REFLECTION

How do you prioritize the needs of others in your relationships?

____

____

____

____

____

____

APPLICATION

Identify one person to honor today and express your appreciation for their role in your life. What did you DO?

____

____

____

Day 6: Peacemaking

Date: _______________________

Matthew 5:9: "God blesses those who work for Peace, for they will be called the children of God."

INSIGHT

As I have gotten older, I have come to understand that being a peace maker does NOT mean keeping the status quo or turning a blind eye to things that are out of place. That is avoidance. Being a peacemaker means confronting those out of place things in love. Peacemaking is a choice to head into uncomfortable places. It takes work and intentionality. As an Ezer, you are called to be a peacemaker, fostering unity and reconciliation in your relationships.

REFLECTION

Where is God calling you to bring peace in your relationships?

____

____

____

____

____

____

APPLICATION

Take one intentional step to promote peace in a strained relationship, whether through prayer, communication, or forgiveness.

____

____

____

____

Day 7: Reflection and Prayer

Date: _________________

REFLECTION

Reflect on how God is shaping you as an Ezer in your relationships. What insights have you gained this week?

____

____

____

____

____

____

PRAYER

Write a prayer asking God to help you embody His love, loyalty, and wisdom in your relationships.

____

____

____

____

____

____

Week 4: Ezer's Role in Community

Learning to live out the call of Ezer to build and strengthen GOD-HONORING COMMUNITIES.

Day 1: Unity in Community

Date: ________________

Acts 2:42-47: *"All the believers devoted themselves to the apostles' teaching, and to fellowship, and to sharing in meals (including the Lord's Supper), and to prayer. A deep sense of awe came over them all, and the apostles performed many miraculous signs and wonders. And all the believers met together in one place and shared everything they had. They sold their property and possessions and shared the money with those in need. They worshiped together at the Temple each day, met in homes for the Lord's Supper, and shared their meals with great joy and generosity - all the while praising God and enjoying the good will of all the people. And each day the Lord added to their fellowship those who were being saved."*

INSIGHT

Early on in my missionary career, I was preparing a team for an outreach in the South of Argentina. Not everyone had the funds to go. Some of the members came from wealthy countries, but the majority did not. As I was praying about how to handle this situation, God brought the above scripture to mind. So, I announced to the team that we were going to put this scripture into practice. I asked that all of us, myself included, put the money that we had together so that we could all go and minister. Those who had very little were all on board, but those few that had greater financial means resisted the idea. We then started to pray for one another, and Holy Spirit turned all our hearts towards unity. We all went. We all had more than enough. We all carried out and completed the mission that God had prepared for us. As Ezers, we play a vital role in fostering unity.

REFLECTION

How can you contribute to building a stronger sense of community?

____

____

____

____

____

____

APPLICATION

Reach out to someone in your church, neighborhood, or circle today and offer encouragement or practical support.

<h1>Day 2: Serving Others</h1>

Date: _______________________

Galatians 5:13: "For you have been called to live in freedom, my brothers and sisters. But don't use your freedom to satisfy your sinful nature. Instead, use your freedom to serve on another in love."

INSIGHT

Sadly, the world we live in today is bent toward serving oneself, looking out for number one. While it is true that we have been given the right of free will. God calls us to use our FREEDOM TO SERVE others in love, reflecting the heart of an Ezer.

REFLECTION

Where is God calling you to serve others?

____

____

____

____

____

____

APPLICATION

Volunteer your time or resources to serve someone in need this week.

Where did you go?

What did you do?

____

____

____

____

Day 3: Bearing Burdens

Date: _____________________

Galatians 6:2: "Share in each other's burdens and in this way obey the law of Christ."

INSIGHT

Bearing one another's burdens fulfills the law of Christ and strengthens the body of Christ.

REFLECTION

How can you support others who are carrying heavy burdens?

____

____

____

____

____

____

____

APPLICATION

Identify one person who may be struggling and offer to pray for or help them in a tangible way. Keep it REAL. Who was it and what did you do for them?

____

____

____

____

____

____

Day 4: Hospitality

Date: _____________________

Romans 12:13: "When God's People are in need, be ready to help them. ALWAYS be eager to practice HOSPITALITY."

INSIGHT

Hospitality is definitely in my wheelhouse. It is my highest-ranking Spiritual gift. I love having people into my home to share Gods Word, a good meal and lots of laughter. It is one of the ways that I show love to and serve others. It is also my way of building community and creating connections for myself and for those who perhaps have few or no connections to speak of. HOSPITALITY reflects God's LOVE and CREATES spaces for COMMUNITY and CONNECTION.

REFLECTION

How can you show hospitality to those around you?

____

____

____

____

____

____

APPLICATION

Host someone for a meal, coffee, or a conversation this week to foster community. Write about that experience.

____

____

____

____

____

Day 5: Encouragement

Date: _________________

Hebrews 10:24-25: "Let us think of ways to motivate one another to acts of LOVE and GOOD WORKS. And let us not NEGLECT our meeting together, as some people do, but ENCOURAGE one another, ESPECIALLY now that the day of HIS return is drawing near."

INSIGHT

I don't know about you, but I sometimes have a penchant for finding lack in the people and things around me. Perhaps this is part of the human condition. Here, Paul instructs us to "think of ways to motivate one another to acts of love and good works." This means that we have to be intentional about it, that this is perhaps something we have lost in our fallen humanity. I have found over the years that encouraging others strengthens their faith and fosters spiritual growth in the community. The act of encouraging others also has the mutual benefit of strengthening my faith and is a source of encouragement to me as well.

REFLECTION

Who in your life needs encouragement today?

____

____

____

____

____

____

APPLICATION

Write a note, send a message, or make a call to encourage someone in their walk with God. In what other practical ways can you encourage others.

____

____

Day 6: Unity in Diversity

Date: _____________________

1 Corinthians 12:12-14: "The human body has many parts, but the many parts make up one whole body. So, it is with the body of Christ. Some of us are Jews, some are Gentiles, some are slaves, and some are free. But we have ALL been baptized into ONE body, by ONE Spirit."

INSIGHT

While diversity has become a "buzz" word to signify the inclusion of different races, ideologies, genders, etc., according to Scripture, diversity is more about how each of us functions as a part of and contributes to the whole. For example, I consider myself a fairly decent writer, but I am not very adept at layout and design. Both are parts of the "whole" of this journal. My friend Chelsea is very gifted at layout and design. If I do the writing and let her do the design, then we model this concept quite nicely. We have different giftings and talents which individually are good, but when we come together and help one another, the whole becomes something great! The body of Christ THRIVES when we embrace diversity and unity, recognizing each person's unique role.

REFLECTION

How can you celebrate the diversity of gifts and perspectives in your community?

____

____

____

____

____

____

____

APPLICATION

Affirm someone's unique gifts or contributions to your community today.

____

____

Date: _____________________

REFLECTION

How has this week deepened your understanding of your role as an Ezer in your community?

____

____

____

____

____

____

PRAYER

Write a prayer asking God to guide you in building stronger, God-centered relationships and communities.

____

____

____

____

____

____

Month 2: Christ's Value for Women

Focuses on how Christ valued and empowered women during His earthly ministry. Through His actions and teachings, Jesus affirmed women's dignity, equality, and vital role in God's kingdom. Each week provides daily reflections that highlight specific encounters, parables, and principles.

Week 1: Christ's Compassion for Women

To reflect on how Jesus CONSISTENTLY showed compassion and care for women, REGARDLESS of societal norms, and discover how we are called to do the same.

Date: _________________________

John 4:4-10: "He had to go through Samaria on the way. Eventually he came to the Samaritan village of Sychar, near the field that Jacob gave his son Joseph. Jacob's well was there; and Jesus, tired from the long walk, sat wearily beside the well about noon-time. Soon a Samaritan woman cane to draw water, and Jesus said to her, 'Please give me a drink.' He was alone at the time because his Disciples had gone into the village to buy some food. The woman was surprised, for Jews refuse to have anything to do with Samaritans. She said to Jesus, 'You are a Jew, and I am a Samaritan woman. Why are you asking me for a drink?' Jesus replied, 'If you only knew the gift God has for you, you would ask me, and I would give you living water.'"

INSIGHT

It is so easy to look at people and judge their actions without knowing who they are, without knowing their story. And let's be honest, we have all been guilty of doing this at one time or another.

Jesus was a Jewish man, speaking to a Samaritan woman in public and in the middle of the day. Because of her lifestyle of going from relationship to relationship, she could not come to the well in the cool of the morning with the other women as she was shunned. Jesus KNEW her story. He UNDERSTOOD her brokenness. Breaking all of the cultural norms of His day, He reaches out to her. His bold act of compassion showed her WORTH despite the cultural norms of the time.

REFLECTION

What barriers might be keeping you from receiving or sharing Christ's compassion?

____

____

____

____

____

____

____

Reflect on a way to show compassion to someone who feels unseen or unworthy.

Day 2: The Woman at the Well (Part 2)

Date: _______________________

John 4:11-26: "But sir, you don't have a rope or a bucket," she said, "and this well is very deep. Where would you get this living water? And besides, do you think you're greater than our ancestor Jacob, who gave us this well? How can you offer better water than he and his sons and his animals enjoyed, Jesus replied, "Anyone who drinks this water will soon become thirsty again. But those who drink the water I give will never be thirsty again. It becomes a fresh bubbling spring within them giving them eternal life." "Please, sir," the woman said, "give me this water! Then I'll never be thirsty again, and I won't have to come here to get water."

"Go and get your husband." Jesus told her. "I don't have a husband," the woman replied. Jesus said, "You're right! You don't have a husband, for you have had five husbands, and you aren't even married to the man you're living with now. You certainly spoke the truth!" "Sir," the woman said, "you must be a prophet. So tell me, why is it you Jews insist that Jerusalem is the only place of worship, while we Samaritans claim it is here at Mount Gerazim, where our ancestors worshipped?"

Jesus replied, "Believe me, dear woman, the time is coming when it will no longer matter whether you worship the Father on this mountain or in Jerusalem. You Samaritans know very little about the one you worship, while we Jews know all about him, for salvation comes through the Jews. But the time is coming - indeed it is here now - when true worshipers will worship the Father in spirit and in truth. The Father is looking for those who will worship him that way. For God is Spirit, so those who worship him must worship him in spirit and in truth."

The woman said, we know the Messiah is coming - the one who is called Christ. When he comes, he will explain everything to us."

Then Jesus told her, "I AM the MESSIAH!"

INSIGHT

Jesus revealed His identity as the Messiah to a Samaritan woman, affirming her VALUE as a recipient of God's truth.

REFLECTION

How does knowing that Christ knows your story and still offers His love impact you?

____

____

____

____

____

____

APPLICATION

Write down one area of your life where you need to accept Christ's unconditional love.

____

____

____

____

____

____

Day 3: The Woman with the Issue of Blood

Date: _________________

Mark 5:25-34: "A woman in the crowd had suffered for twelve years with constant bleeding. She had suffered a great deal with many doctors, and over the years she had spent everything she had to pay them, but she had gotten no better. In fact, she had gotten worse. She had heard about Jesus, so she came up behind him through the crowd and touched his robe. For she thought to herself, 'If I can just touch his robe, I will be healed.' Immediately, the bleeding stopped, and she could feel in her body that she had been healed of her terrible condition. Jesus realized at once that healing power had gone out from him, so he turned around in the crowd and asked, 'Who touched my robe?' His disciples said to him, 'Look at this crowd pressing around you. How can you ask, 'Who touched me?' But he kept on looking around to see who had done it. Then the frightened woman, trembling at the realization of what had happened to her, came and fell to her knees in front of him and told him what she had done. And he said to her, 'Daughter, your faith has made you well. Go in peace. Your suffering is over.'"

INSIGHT

Have you ever suffered with any type of chronic condition? I have. From the time I was a teenager, I suffered from chronic depression. I too had spent a considerable amount of time, effort, and money on counseling and this anti-depressant or that. I had been in ministry for many years and the fact that nothing seemed to permanently lift me out of those dark places, was a source of great shame for me. On May 8, 2022, Mother's Day, I had finally had enough of life and did not want to go on living. I was forced into being admitted to a mental healthcare facility. It was in that place that Jesus touched me and helped me to see that I had been looking to others, rather than Him to heal my soul. It was there that He helped me to give those wounds to Him and allow Him to carry that load. Today, I do not use any medication and have not been depressed in more than three years. Like the woman with the issue of blood, Jesus healed my suffering, affirmed my faith, carried away my shame, and began restoring my identity in HIM.

REFLECTION

How does Christ's willingness to stop for this woman encourage you to bring your needs to Him?

____

____

____

____

APPLICATION

Write a prayer asking Christ to meet a specific need in your life today.

Day 4: The Widow of Nain

Date: _________________

Luke 7:11-17: "Soon afterward Jesus went with his disciples to the village of Nain and a large crowd followed him. A funeral procession was coming out as he approached the village gate. The young man who had died was a widow's only son, and a large crowd from the village was with her. When the Lord saw her, his heart overflowed with compassion. 'Don't cry!' he said. Then he walked over to the coffin and touched it and the bearers stopped. 'Young man!' he said, 'I tell you to get up.' Then the dead boy sat up and began to talk! And Jesus gave him back to his mother. Great fear swept through the crowd, and they praised God saying, 'A mighty prophet has risen among us,' and 'God has visited his people today.' And the news about Jesus spread throughout Judea and the surrounding countryside.'"

INSIGHT

The word compassion comes from the Latin word *compassio*. It means to suffer together. This passage says that Jesus' "heart OVERFLOWED with compassion." He shared a deep awareness of her suffering and desired to alleviate that suffering. Jesus had compassion for this grieving widow and restored her hope by raising her son from the dead. We were NEVER meant to be left suffering in solitude. As Ezers, we must come to a place of receiving Christ's compassion towards us and allow Him to walk with us in our sufferings. In turn, we must also come to the place where we purposefully do the same for others.

REFLECTION

How has Christ's compassion brought healing or hope in your life?

____

____

____

____

____

____

____

APPLICATION

Look for someone in your community who may need comfort and reach out to them with a kind gesture or prayer.

____

____

____

____

____

____

Day 5: Mary and Martha's Grief

Date: ______________________

John 11:32-36: When Mary arrived and saw Jesus, she fell at his feet and said, 'Lord, if only you had been here, my brother would not have died.' When Jesus saw her weeping and saw the other people wailing with her, a deep anger welled up within him and he was deeply troubled. 'Where have you put him?' he asked them. They told him, 'Lord come and see.' Then Jesus wept. The people who were standing nearby said, 'See how much he loved him!'"

INSIGHT

About six months after my first husband died, I had a compassionate encounter with Jesus. During a grief counseling session, I had a vision that I will never forget. At one point, as my counselor, Eric, was ministering to me, he bent over and laid hands on my feet. Eric had light-colored eyes, but when he looked up at me, his eye color turned to the warmest, liquid brown I had ever seen. In my spirit I recognized that Jesus was looking at me with deep compassion, through Eric's eyes. The warmth that I felt at that moment was indescribable. My whole being, was flooded with a deep understanding that in my loss, Jesus was with me. In much the same way, Jesus wept with Mary and Martha before raising Lazarus, showing His deep empathy and care for their pain.

REFLECTION

How does knowing Jesus grieves with you bring you comfort?

____

____

____

____

____

APPLICATION

Write down one way you can show empathy to someone experiencing pain or loss.

____

____

Day 6: Forgiveness for the Sinful Woman

Date: _________________

Luke 7:36-50: "One of the Pharisees asked Jesus to have dinner with him, so Jesus went to his home and sat down to eat. When a certain immoral woman from that city heard he was eating there, she brought a beautiful alabaster jar filled with expensive perfume. Then she knelt behind him at his feet, weeping. Her tears fell on his feet, and she wiped them off with her hair. Then she kept kissing his feet and putting perfume on them. When the Pharisee who invited him saw this, he said to himself, 'If this man were a prophet, he would know what kind of woman is touching him. She's a sinner!' Then Jesus answered his thoughts, 'Simon,' he said to the Pharisee, 'I have something to say to you.' 'Go ahead, Teacher.' Simon replied. Then Jesus told him this story: 'A man loaned money to two people - 500 pieces of silver to one and 50 pieces to the other. But neither of them could repay him, so he kindly forgave them both, canceling their debts. Who do you suppose loved him more after that?' Simon answered, 'I suppose the one for whom he cancelled the larger debt.' 'That's right,' Jesus said. Then he turned to the woman and said to Simon, 'Look at this woman kneeling here. When I entered your home, you didn't offer me water to wash the dust from my feet, but she has washed them with her tears and wiped them with her hair. You didn't greet me with a kiss, but from the time I first came in, she has not stopped kissing my feet. You neglected the courtesy of olive oil to anoint my head, but she has anointed my feet with rare perfume. I tell you her sins have been forgiven, so she has shown me much love. But a person who is forgiven little shows only little love.' Then Jesus said to the woman, ' Your sins are forgiven.' The men at the table said among themselves, 'Who is this man that he goes around forgiving sins?' And Jesus said to the woman. 'Your faith has saved you; go in peace.'"

INSIGHT

Jesus forgave and honored a sinful woman who anointed His feet, demonstrating the depth of His grace and love. Do we demonstrate His grace and love in the same manner? Or are we like Simon, who although He did not say it, His thoughts and opinions about the woman's shamefully sinful state were heard.

REFLECTION

How does Christ's forgiveness free you from shame?

____

____

____

____

____

____

_______________________________________ 82

APPLICATION

Write down one way you can extend forgiveness to yourself or someone else today.

____

____

____

____

____

____

Day 7: Reflection and Prayer

Date: _______________

REFLECTION

What have you learned this week about Christ's compassion and care for women?

____

____

____

____

____

____

PRAYER

Write a prayer thanking Jesus for His compassion and asking Him to help you reflect His love to others.

____

____

____

____

____

____

Week 2: Christ's Empowerment of Women

To examine how Jesus EMPOWERED women by teaching, healing, and INVOLVING them in His ministry.

Day 1: Mary, Mother of Jesus

Date: _______________

Luke 1:26-38: 'In the sixth month of Elizabeth's pregnancy, God sent the angel Gabriel to Nazareth, a village in Galilee, to a virgin named Mary. She was engaged to be married to a man named Joseph, a descendant of King David. Gabriel appeared to her and said, 'Greetings favored Woman! The Lord is with you!' Confused and disturbed, Mary tried to think of what the Angel could mean. 'Don't be afraid Mary,' the angel told her, 'For you have found favor with God!! You will conceive and give birth to a son, and you will name him Jesus. He will be very great and will be called the Son of the Most High. The Lord God will give him the throne of his ancestor David. And he will reign over Israel forever; his Kingdom will never end!' Mary asked the angel, 'But how can this happen? I am a virgin.' The angel replied, 'The Holy Spirit will come upon you, and the power of the Most High will overshadow you. So, the baby to be born will be holy, and he will be called the Son of God. What's more, your relative Elizabeth has become pregnant in her old age! People used to say she was barren, but she has conceived a son and is now in her sixth month. For the word of God will never fail.' Mary responded, 'I am the Lord's servant. May everything you have said about me come true.' And then the angel left her.'"

INSIGHT

Do you struggle with the thought of having been chosen by God to fulfill His divine purposes? If we are honest, I think we all do. When God gave me the assignment to write this journal, I wondered what I could have to say that would make any lasting impact on anyone. "Who am I that anyone would even listen?" He gently and lovingly reminded me that the task was not about what I had to say, or who I was, but it was about who He is and what He had to say through me. Humility check? Absolutely! Mary was just a simple girl. Yet, God chose Mary to bear His Son, EMPOWERING her to fulfill her divine purpose DESPITE her youth and low status. May we all say like Mary, "I am the Lord's servant. May everything you have said about me come true."

REFLECTION

How does God's choice of Mary encourage you to trust Him with your calling?

____

____

____

____

____

APPLICATION

Write down one way you feel God is calling you to serve Him today.

Date: _______________________

Luke 10:38-42: "As Jesus and the disciples continued on their way to Jerusalem, they came to a certain village where a woman named Martha welcomed him into her home. Her sister, Mary, sat at the Lord's feet, listening to what he taught. But Martha was distracted by the big dinner she was preparing. She came to Jesus and said, 'Lord, doesn't it seem unfair to you that my sister just sits here while I do all of the work? Tell her to come and help me.' But the Lord said to her, 'My dear Martha, you are worried and upset over all these details! There is only one thing worth being concerned about. Mary has discovered it. And it will not be taken away from her.'"

INSIGHT

Mary sat at Jesus' feet, breaking cultural NORMS to learn from Him as His disciple. Jesus AFFIRMED her choice. For women today in the United States, the norm is to be busy ALL THE TIME. Work, ministry, homemaking, school, spouses, children, and even church "activities," can cause us to feel like Martha; like it's too much. At the end of the day, all of those things can be taken from us. When we are consumed with things that are temporal, we can miss the most important thing, which is to sit at His feet, to learn from Him, to allow Him to ease our stress and carry our burdens. Once we discover that, no one can ever take it away from us.

REFLECTION

How can you prioritize sitting at Jesus' feet amid the busyness of life?

____

____

____

____

____

APPLICATION

Set aside 15 minutes today to meditate on God's Word and listen to His voice.

____

Day3: Mary of Bethany (Part 2)

Date: _________________

John 12:1-3: 'Six days before the Passover celebration began, Jesus arrived in Bethany, the home of Lazarus - the man he had raised from the dead. A dinner was prepared in Jesus' honor. Martha served and Lazarus was among those who ate with him. Then Mary took a twelve-ounce jar of expensive perfume made from essence of nard, and she anointed Jesus' feet with it, wiping his feet with her hair. The house was filled with the fragrance."

INSIGHT

Mary's anointing of Jesus demonstrated her devotion and understanding of His mission. It was an extravagant expression of love and gratitude. In our last look at Mary of Bethany, we looked at how life's innumerable distractions can lead us to miss out on the blessing it is to just sit at Jesus' feet. But this is only one side of the coin. When we make the conscious choice to get off the hamster wheel and sit with him, in worship, reading scripture, or just basking in His presence, what we are really doing is anointing Him with the perfume of our time and our hearts. We bless Him. We honor Him. We please Him. Unlike Mary's perfume, worth one year's wages, our time spent with Him is priceless.

REFLECTION

How can you show extravagant love for Christ in your daily life?

____

____

____

____

____

____

APPLICATION

Choose one way to express your love for Christ today, whether through worship, service, or giving.

Day 4: The Canaanite Woman

Date: ________________

Matthew 15:21-28: "Then Jesus left Galilee and went north to the region of Tyre and Sidon. A Gentile woman who lived there came to him, pleading, 'Have mercy on me, O lord, Son of David! For my daughter is possessed by a demon that torments her severely." But Jesus gave her no reply, not even a word. Then his disciples urged him to send her away. 'Tell her to go away,' they said. 'She is bothering us with all her begging.' Then Jesus said to the woman, 'I was sent only to help God's lost sheep - the people of Israel.' But she came and worshiped him, pleading again, 'Lord help me!' Jesus responded, 'It isn't right to take food from the children and throw it to the dogs.' She replied, 'That's true, Lord, but even dogs are allowed to eat the scraps that fall beneath their master's table.' 'Dear woman,' Jesus said to her, 'your faith is great. Your request is granted.' And her daughter was instantly healed."

INSIGHT

There are several very close loved ones in my life that even though they know the truth of the God's word, they have gotten swept up into this world's way of doing life. They are not walking In God's ways, and quite honestly seem to have lost interest in even doing so. Time and time again I have tried to help them back to His paths to no avail. I shared scripture, teachings, etcetera, and still nada. I had begun to lose hope that they ever would. I began praying for them, which is where I should have started in the first place. When I started doing this consistently, two things happened. First, I began to have hope again that in God's timing, they would come back to him. God says that His word doesn't go forth without completing the purpose for which it was sent. (Isaiah 55:11) Second, I began to see them and myself from a different perspective. HIS. As crazy as it sounds, I had gotten wrapped up into thinking that this was a work that I had to complete. But it is Holy Spirit who holds the power to transform lives, not me. The more I got that truth into my heart, the more I could see glimpses of Jesus working in their hearts and minds. Glimmers of hope that became renewed faith that one day, HE will heal their hearts, lead them to repentance and bring them back to His side.

REFLECTION

How can persistence in prayer strengthen your faith?

____

____

____

____

____

____

____

____

APPLICATION

Write a prayer of faith for a specific situation, trusting God's power and timing.

____

____

____

____

____

____

____

Day 5: Women Witnesses to the Resurrection

Date: _________________

Matthew 28:1-10: "Early on Sunday morning, as the new day was dawning, Mary Magdalene and the other Mary went out to visit the tomb. Suddenly there was a great earthquake! For an angel of the Lord came down from Heaven, rolled aside the stone, and sat on it. His face shone like lightning, and his clothing was as white as snow. The guards shook with fear when they saw him, and they fell into a dead faint. Then the angel spoke to the women, 'Don't be afraid!' he said, 'I know you are looking for Jesus, who was crucified. He isn't here! He is risen from the dead, and he is going ahead, of you to Galilee. You will see him there. Remember what I have told you.' The women ran quickly from the tomb. They were very frightened but also filled with great Joy, and they rushed to give the disciples the angel's message. And as they went, Jesus met them and greeted them. And they ran to him, grasped his feet and worshipped him. Then Jesus said to them. 'Don't be afraid! Go tell my brothers to leave for Galilee, and they will see me there.'"

INSIGHT

The angel did not announce to the rulers of the day that Jesus had risen from the dead. He did not appear to Jesus' inner circle—Peter, James, and John. Instead, two women were the FIRST witnesses to Jesus' resurrection. This broke all the social constructs of the day and the culture. It is no wonder that the disciples did not believe them without first going to see for themselves. What is more amazing to me is that the disciples, who had been with Jesus for three years, had been told that this was how things would unfold. So had the women. The angel said to them, "Remember what I have told you." Yet it was Mary Magdalene and Mary, the mother of James, who believed the angel without question. They did not even see Jesus until they were running back to tell the disciples the GOOD NEWS. Women were the first commissioned to share the Gospel.

REFLECTION

How does Jesus' trust in these women inspire your confidence to share the Gospel?

____

____

____

____

____

APPLICATION

Share an encouraging Scripture or testimony with someone today.

____

____

____

____

____

____

Date: ________________

Luke 8:1-3: "Soon afterword Jesus began a tour of the nearby towns and villages, preaching and announcing the Good News about the Kingdom of God. He took his twelve Disciples with him, along with some women who had been cured of evil spirits and Diseases. Among them were Mary Magdalene, from whom he had cast out seven Demons, Joanna, the wife of Chuza, Herod's business manager; Susanna; and many others who were contributing from their own resources to support Jesus and his disciples."

INSIGHT

It is interesting to note that it was not male captains of industry who would financially support Jesus' ministry, but women. Joanna and Susanna supported Jesus' ministry with their resources, playing a vital role in His work. In their "unconventional" role, the Scripture highlights women's essential importance in furthering the Gospel and the Kingdom.

REFLECTION

How can you use your resources to further God's kingdom?

____

____

____

____

____

____

____

APPLICATION

Identify one way to give your time, talent, or treasure to support God's work this week.

____

____

____

Date: _______________________

REFLECTION

How has Jesus' empowerment of women encouraged you to step into your calling?

____

____

____

____

____

____

PRAYER

Write a prayer asking God to empower you to serve Him boldly and faithfully.

____

____

____

____

____

____

Week 3: Christ's Teachings About Love and Faith

To explore and ponder how Jesus used parables to teach about God's love, faith, and redemption, inviting both men and women to embrace His message and live by it.

Day 1: The Parable of the Lost Sheep

Date: ___________________

Luke 15:1-7: "Tax collectors and other notorious sinners often came to listen to Jesus teach. This made the Pharisees and teachers of religious law complain that he was associating with such sinful people - even eating with them! So, Jesus told them this story: 'If a man has a hundred sheep and one of them gets lost, what will he do? Won't he leave the ninety-nine others in the wilderness to go and search for the one that is lost until he finds it? And when he has found it, he will joyfully carry it home on his shoulders. When he arrives, he will call together his friends and neighbors saying, 'Rejoice with me because I have found my lost sheep.' In the same way, there is more joy in heaven over one lost sinner who repents and returns to God than over ninety-nine others who are righteous and haven't strayed away!"

INSIGHT

I love this image; it is the image of Jesus pursuing you and me. The most basic definition of the word pursuit is the act of "chasing" after someone or something. This isn't just a casual "look see," like when you send one of your kiddos to get something for you and two seconds later, after having glanced in the general area of where said object should be, you hear "where is it mom? I can't find it." No, this is more like treasure hunters seeking lost and all but forgotten fortunes. They go to any length and leave no stone unturned until they find the treasure they seek. God displayed the ultimate pursuit of His creation sending His only Son to be born as a baby, crucified and buried as a man, and resurrected as our eternal Savior. The GOD OF THE UNIVERSE pursues you and I every single moment of every single day. Jesus taught that God values EVERY person and REJOICES when one who is lost returns to Him.

REFLECTION

In what ways have you experienced God's relentless pursuit of you?

____

____

____

____

____

____

APPLICATION

Spend time praying for someone in your life who may feel far from God and ask Him to use you to show His love.

____

____

____

____

____

____

____

Date: ___________________

Luke 15:8-10: "Or suppose a woman has ten silver coins and loses one. Won't she light a lamp and sweep the entire house and search for it carefully until she finds it? And when she finds it, she will call in her friends and neighbors and say, 'Rejoice with me because I have found my lost coin.' In the same way there is joy in the presence of God's angels when even one sinner repents"

INSIGHT

I remember once when I was preparing for a mission deployment in South America. I had carefully put my passport in a place where I would remember where it was. The morning, I was supposed to leave, in my excitement, I could not remember where I had placed it!! If I couldn't find it, there would be no trip and missed opportunities to share the Gospel with those God had called me to. I searched franticly but could not find it anywhere in that little six-hundred square foot apartment. I called my friend and pastor's wife Teresa and told her about it. She stopped and prayed with me. Suddenly, I could envision exactly where my passport was. I found the figurative "X," and in that spot, found the treasure that was my passport. I called Theresa back and told her that I had found it. Needless to say, a serious happy dance then ensued on both ends!! That is just a fraction of the joy that I think God must feel when just one of us repents and comes to him.

REFLECTION

How do you celebrate the small victories of faith in your life or others?

____

____

____

____

____

____

APPLICATION

Write a prayer of thanksgiving for God's persistent love in your life.

Day 3: The Parable of the Prodigal Son (Part 1)

Date: _________________

Luke 15:11-24: Then He said: "A certain man had two sons. And the younger of them said to his father, 'Father, give me the portion of goods that falls to me.' So he divided to them his livelihood. And not many days after, the younger son gathered all together, journeyed to a far country, and there wasted his possessions with prodigal living. But when he had spent all, there arose a severe famine in that land, and he began to be in want. Then he went and joined himself to a citizen of that country, and he sent him into his fields to feed swine. And he would gladly have filled his stomach with the pods that the swine ate, and no one gave him anything.

"But when he came to himself, he said, 'How many of my father's hired servants have bread enough and to spare, and I perish with hunger! I will arise and go to my father, and will say to him, "Father, I have sinned against heaven and before you, and I am no longer worthy to be called your son. Make me like one of your hired servants."

And he arose and came to his father. But when he was still a great way off, his father saw him and had compassion, and ran and fell on his neck and kissed him. And the son said to him, "Father, I have sinned against heaven and in your sight, and am no longer worthy to be called your son."

But the father said to his servants, "Bring out the best robe and put it on him, and put a ring on his hand and sandals on his feet. And bring the fatted calf here and kill it, and let us eat and be merry; for this my son was dead and is alive again; he was lost and is found." And they began to be merry.

INSIGHT

"And while he was still a long way off, his father saw him coming." Let that sink in for a moment. This son had everything and threw it all away. He knew the goodness of his father's household but turned his back on it. His son's actions were disrespectful and showed a serious lack of gratitude towards his father and the sacrifices he had made to provide for him. And what does his father do... he waits, and waits, and waits, every day with great expectation that his ungrateful son should return to him. And then he runs to him, welcomes him, and throws a celebration for him!!! Why? The simple answer is because of his love for his son. In this story, Jesus revealed God's love for the wayward and His eagerness to forgive and restore.

REFLECTION

How does this parable speak to God's mercy in your life?

____

____

____

____

____

APPLICATION

Identify one area of your life where you need God's forgiveness.

Write it down and surrender it to Him in prayer.

____

____

____

____

____

____

Day 4: The Parable of the Prodigal Son (Part 2)

Date: ________________

Luke 15:25-32: Meanwhile the older son was in the fields working. When he returned home, he heard music and dancing in the house, and he asked one of the servants what was going on. 'Your brother is back' he was told, 'and your father has killed the fattened calf. We are celebrating because of his safe return.' The older brother was angry and wouldn't go in. His father came out and begged him, but he replied, 'All these years I've slaved for you and never once refused to do a single thing you told me to. And in all that time you never even gave me one young goat for a feast with my friends. Yet when this son of yours comes back after squandering your money on prostitutes, you celebrate by killing the fattened calf!' His father said to him, 'Look, dear son, you have always stayed by me, and everything I have is yours. We had to celebrate this happy day. For your brother was dead and has come back to life! He was lost, but no he is found!"

INSIGHT

In this parable, the focus of most of the messages, teachings and preachings that I have ever heard are on the prodigal, the son who leaves. But what about the son that stayed? He served. He never refused to do anything that was asked of him. He followed the rules of his household. In his mind and in his heart, he had done everything right. But when his brother returns and a HUGE deal is made by the father, he feels cheated. The elder brother struggles to understand the father's extravagant display of grace towards the wayward son. I think he must have wondered how the father could forgive the prodigal so easily. Jesus uses this parable to highlight the JOY of forgiveness because His mission was to restore our relationship with God the Father.

REFLECTION

Have you ever struggled to celebrate God's blessings in someone else's life?

____

____

____

____

____

____

APPLICATION

Celebrate someone's success today, whether it's through a word of encouragement or a prayer of gratitude on their behalf.

____

____

____

____

____

____

Day 5: The Persistent Widow

Date: _______________________

Luke 18:1-8: "One day Jesus told his disciples a story to show that they should always pray and never give up. 'There was a judge in a certain city' he said, 'who neither feared God nor cared about people. A widow of that city came to him repeatedly saying, 'Give me justice in this dispute with my enemy.' The judge ignored her for a while, but finally he said to himself, 'I don't fear God or care about people, but this woman is driving me crazy. I'm going to see that she gets justice, because she is wearing me out with her constant requests.' Then the Lord said, 'Learn a lesson from this unjust judge. Even he rendered a just decision in the end. So, don't you think God will surely give justice to his chosen people who cry out to him day and night? Will he keep putting them off? I tell you he will grant justice to them quickly! But when the Son of Man returns, how many will he find on the earth who have faith?'"

INSIGHT

When I was about 12 years old, I REALLY wanted a pair of roller skates with wooden wheels. They were in vogue at the time. So, I asked my mom if she would buy them for me. She was a single widow, so money was tight. The skates were only thirty dollars, but that was a considerable amount of groceries. She made a deal with me, if I would save up half of the money, she would save the other half and then we would buy them. For weeks I consistently saved my allowance and did chores for neighbors. A quarter here or a dollar there; anything to have those skates. Finally, when I had saved up my half, and she hers, we went and bought them as she had promised. I was so proud of them. Just like the widow pestered the judge until she received the justice she desired, I believed my mama when she promised that if I would do my part, she would do hers. The widow also believed, and God delivered in her situation. The story of this widow illustrates the importance of CONSISTENT prayer and faith.

REFLECTION

Where do you need to persevere in prayer today?

____

____

____

____

____

APPLICATION

Write down a specific prayer request and commit to praying persistently for it over the coming weeks.

____

____

____

____

____

____

Day 6: The Mustard Seed and Yeast

Date: _________________

Matthew 13:31-33: "Here is another illustration Jesus used: 'The Kingdom of Heaven is like a mustard seed planted in a field. It is the smallest of all seeds, but it becomes the largest of garden plants; it grows into a tree, and birds come and make nests in its branches.' Jesus also used this illustration: 'The Kingdom of Heaven is like the yeast a woman used in making bread. Even though she put only a little yeast in three measures of flour, it permeated every part of the dough.'"

INSIGHT

Have you ever wondered what it means to have GREAT faith? Have you ever said to yourself, I wish I had big faith like this or that person? I know I have. Romans 12:3 teaches that God is the one who gives each of us a specific measure of faith. It is not something that we can manufacture for ourselves. Faith is a divine gift that He gives to all of us. It takes faith to believe that Jesus would die for us, or even that we needed Him to, and in turn accept that gift. Every time we believe God for something, that faith grows. I think that how much faith we have, if that can even be measured, is directly related to the specific plan and mission that God has for each one of us. Here, Jesus compares faith and the kingdom of God to a mustard seed and yeast to illustrate how SMALL beginnings can grow into GREAT exploits for the Kingdom.

REFLECTION

Where is God asking you to trust Him for growth in your life?

____

____

____

____

____

____

APPLICATION

Take one small step of faith today toward something God has placed on your heart. Record what that was.

Day 7: Reflection and Prayer

Date: _________________

REFLECTION

How have Jesus' parables deepened your understanding of God's love and your faith?

____

____

____

____

____

____

PRAYER

Write a prayer thanking God for His love and asking Him to strengthen your faith.

____

____

____

____

____

____

____

Week 4: Christ's Interactions with Women

We will study Jesus' compassion, healing, and acknowledgment of women in moments of profound significance. Jesus' interactions with women highlights our value, faith, and unique roles in God's kingdom.

Day 1: The Healing of the Bleeding Woman

Date: ________________________

Mark 5:25-34: "A woman in the crowd had suffered for twelve years with constant bleeding. She had suffered a great deal with many doctors, and over the years she had spent everything she had to pay them, but she had gotten no better. In fact, she had gotten worse. She had heard about Jesus, so she came up behind him through the crowd and touched his robe. For she thought to herself, 'If I can just touch his robe, I will be healed.' Immediately the bleeding stopped, and she could feel in her body that she had been healed of her terrible condition. Jesus realized at once that Healing power had gone out from him, so he turned around in the crowd and asked, 'Who touched my robe?' His disciples said to him. 'Look at this crowd pressing around you. How can you ask, 'Who touched me?' But he kept on looking around to see who had done it. Then the frightened woman, trembling at the realization of what had happened to her, came and fell to her knees in front of him and told him what she had done. And he said to her, 'Daughter, your faith has made you well. Go in peace. Your suffering is over.'"

INSIGHT

There is a real hurdle between us and God. Sin. Just like this woman's issue of blood, our sin makes us unclean and unable to enter into the presence of a Holy God. We are "bleeding out" if you will. Many of us have looked for our significance in so many other things and at great cost.

Jesus healed this woman who had suffered for 12 years and called her "DAUGHTER," affirming her faith and dignity. When we come to Him and acknowledge our need for healing and forgiveness of our sin, He recognizes our faith, restores our dignity, and gives us a new identity as DAUGHTERS!

REFLECTION

How does Jesus' willingness to meet the needs of this woman encourage you to approach Him with your struggles?

____

____

____

____

____

APPLICATION

Identify a personal challenge you've been hesitant to bring to Jesus. Write a prayer of faith, trusting Him to meet your need.

Day 2: Jesus and the Samaritan Woman (Part 1)

Date: _________________

John 4:1-15: "Jesus knew that the Pharisees had heard that he was baptizing and making more disciples than John (though Jesus himself didn't baptize them - his disciples did). So, he left Judea and returned to Galilee. He had to go through Samaria on the way. Eventually he came to the Samarian village of Sychar, near the field that Jacob gave to his son Joseph. Jacob's well was there; and Jesus, tired from the long walk, sat wearily beside the well about noontime. Soon a Samaritan woman came to draw water, and Jesus said to her, 'Please give me a drink.' Jesus was alone at the time because his disciples had gone to the village to buy some food. The woman was surprised, for Jews refuse to have anything to do with Samaritans. She said to Jesus, 'You are a Jew, and I am a Samaritan woman. Why are you asking me for a drink?' Jesus replied, 'If you only knew the gift God has for you and who you are speaking to, you would ask me, and I would give you living water.' 'But sir, you don't have a rope or a bucket.' she said, 'and this well is very deep. Where would you get this living water? And besides, do you think you are better than our ancestor Jacob. Who gave us this well? How can you offer better water than he and his sons and his animals enjoyed?' Jesus replied, 'Anyone who drinks this water will soon be thirsty again. But those who drink the water I give will never be thirsty again. It becomes a fresh, bubbling spring within them, giving them eternal life.'"

INSIGHT

I don't know where God initiates conversations with you? For me it is usually when I am doing something pretty mundane, like washing the dishes, folding laundry or just driving in my car. The most common, though most unexpected, place is in my bathroom while taking a shower or other bathroom things. I have often wondered why this is. In light of this particular parable, perhaps it is because in the natural world, the bathroom is where we go for daily cleansing. The Samaritan woman wasn't doing anything special that day. She was just doing what she did every day. Jesus however did something totally out of character for their cultural context. He met with her where she least expected. She was dry and thirsty and was there for physical water. That day, she left with living water and the promise that she would NEVER be thirsty again.

REFLECTION

How does knowing that Jesus offers you living water (eternal life) shape your understanding of your worth in Him?

____

____

____

____

____

____

____

APPLICATION

Spend time reflecting on areas of your life that feel "dry" and ask Jesus to fill them with His living water.

____

____

____

____

____

____

Day 3: Jesus and the Samaritan Woman (Part 2)

Date: _________________

John 4:16-30: "Go and get your husband.' Jesus told her. 'I don't have a husband,' the woman replied. Jesus said, 'You're right! You don't have a husband, for you have had five husbands, and you aren't even married to the man you're living with now. You certainly spoke the truth!' 'Sir," the woman said, 'you must be a prophet. So, tell me why it is that you Jews insist that Jerusalem is the only place of worship, while we Samaritans claim it is here at Mount Gerazim, where our ancestors worshiped?' Jesus replied, 'Believe me, dear woman, the time is coming when it will no longer matter whether you worship the Father on this mountain or in Jerusalem. You Samaritans know very little about the one you worship, while we Jews know all about him, for salvation comes through the Jews. But the time is coming, indeed it's here now, when true worshipers will worship the Father in spirit and in truth. The Father is looking for those who will worship Him that way. For God is Spirit, so those who worship him must worship in spirit and in truth.' The woman said, I know the Messiah is coming - the one who is called Christ. When he comes, he will explain everything to us.' Then Jesus told her, 'I am the Messiah!' Just then his disciples came back. They were shocked to find him talking to a woman, but none of them had the nerve to ask, 'What do you want with her?' or 'Why are you talking to her?' The woman left her water jar beside the well and ran back to the village, telling everyone, 'Come and see a man who told me everything I ever did! Could he possibly be the Messiah?' So, the people came streaming from the village to see him."

INSIGHT

Her village saw only her brokenness, but Jesus saw her potential in His Kingdom. Jesus revealed the truth of her life, but did so with compassion, drawing her into deeper understanding and a restored purpose. I love that He sees both in me as well. It makes me feel humbled, worthy, and truly seen.

REFLECTION

How does Jesus' ability to see both your brokenness and potential make you feel?

____

____

____

____

____

____

____

APPLICATION

Write down one way you feel called to share the hope of Christ with others this week.

____

____

____

____

____

____

Day 4: The Woman Caught in Adultery

Date: ________________

John 8:1-11: 'Jesus returned to the Mount of Olives, but early the next morning he was back again at the Temple. A crowd soon gathered, and he sat down and taught them. As he was speaking, the teachers of religious law and the Pharisees brought a woman who had been caught in the act of adultery. They put her in front of the crowd. 'Teacher,' they said to Jesus, 'this woman was caught in the act of adultery. The law of Moses says to stone her. What do you say?' They were trying to trap him into saying something they could use against him, but Jesus stooped down and wrote in the dust with his finger. They kept demanding an answer, so he stood up again and said, 'All right, but let the one who has never sinned throw the first stone!' Then he stooped down again and wrote in the dust. When the accusers heard this, they slipped away one by one, beginning with the oldest, until only Jesus was left in the middle of the crowd with the woman. Then Jesus stood up again and said to the woman, 'Where are your accusers? Didn't even one of them condemn you?' 'No, Lord,' she said. And Jesus said, 'Neither do I. Go and sin no more.'"

INSIGHT

Jesus protected this woman caught in adultery from condemnation and extended forgiveness, calling her to leave her life of sin. It is the same call he has for all of us. Do you ever wonder what happened after she left him? Did she ever do it again? Did others still see her as she had been completely missing who she now was? Did she ever become her own accuser, struggling to fully embrace the GRACE that had been extended to her? If she is anything like me, the answer is probably a big YES! Sometimes, I struggle to walk in the freedom of His forgiveness, remembering who I was and forgetting who I now am in Christ. Do you?

REFLECTION

How does Jesus' grace toward this woman encourage you to embrace His forgiveness and walk in freedom?

____

____

____

____

____

APPLICATION

Identify one area of your life where you need to fully accept God's grace. Write a prayer of surrender and gratitude.

____

____

____

____

____

____

Day 5: The Women Called by Jesus

Date: _______________________

Luke 8:1-3: "Soon afterward Jesus began a tour of the nearby towns and villages, preaching and announcing the Good News about the Kingdom of God. He took his twelve disciples with him, along with some women who had been cured of evil spirits and diseases. Among them were Mary Magdalene, from whom he had cast out seven demons; Joanna, the wife of Chuza, Herod's business manager; Susanna; and many others who were contributing from their own resources to support Jesus and his disciples."

INSIGHT

We have looked at this before and talked about these ladies' active roles in Jesus' ministry. They wanted to support what He was doing. But Mary Magdalene, Joanna, and Susanna didn't just follow Jesus. The scripture says that Jesus "took" them along with Him. They were CALLED to be with Him just as much as any of the twelve disciples. WOW! Let that sink in... These ladies were not secondary to the twelve in Jesus' mission while on earth. They were counterparts to them. The truth is, so are YOU!

REFLECTION

How does Jesus' calling these women to play a vital role in His ministry impact how you see your role as an active participant God's Kingdom work today?

____

____

____

____

____

____

APPLICATION

Spend some time with Jesus and ask Him to show you one thing this week that He is calling you to do to take an active role in furthering His Kingdom. You have a mission to complete, so make sure to listen for your calling.

Day 6: Women at the Cross

Date: _______________________

Matthew 27:55-56: "And many women who had come from Galilee with Jesus to care for him were watching from a distance. Among them were Mary Magdalene, (the mother of James and Joseph), and the mother of James and John, the sons of Zebedee."

INSIGHT

It was the worst day of their lives!! The man that they had sacrificed so much for, was now being sacrificed for them. Crucifixion was reserved for the worst of criminals, but what had Jesus done? I can't imagine the confusion, pain, and perhaps anger they must have felt. But there they were in Jesus' last moments on earth. And where were the men? Where were the twelve that had traveled and ministered with Him for three years? The answer... most of Jesus' disciples fled during His crucifixion. But the women remained at the cross. In the midst of the unimaginable, the women remained, showing their FAITHFULNESS and COURAGE.

REFLECTION

How does the faithfulness of these women inspire you to stand firm in your own faith?

____

____

____

____

____

____

APPLICATION

Write a prayer asking God for the courage to remain steadfast in difficult times.

____

____

____

Day 7: Reflection and Prayer

Date: _________________

REFLECTION

Reflect on how Jesus' interactions with women in this week's studies have deepened your understanding of His care, compassion, and empowerment.

____

____

____

____

____

____

PRAYER

Write a prayer thanking Jesus for the ways He affirmed and valued women during His ministry. Ask Him to help you live out your faith with courage and compassion, just as these women did.

____

____

____

____

____

____

APPLICATION

Share a story or insight from this week with someone who might need encouragement about their worth in Christ. Write it down then share the GOOD NEWS!

____

Month 3: Walking in the Power of the Holy Spirit

This month focuses on how understanding God's love and Christ's value for women equipping us to walk in the power of the Holy Spirit. Through the Spirit, we are empowered to live boldly, embrace our purpose, and foster community. Each week explores how the Holy Spirit works in our lives to bear fruit, guide us in truth, and empower us for kingdom work.

Week 1: The Gift of the Holy Spirit

To understand the role of the Holy Spirit in the life of the believer and how He empowers us to live out our CALLING.

Day 1: The Promise of the Holy Spirit

Date: ________________

John 14:16-17: "And I will ask the Father, and he will give you another Advocate, who will never leave you. He is the Holy Spirit, who leads us into all truth. The world cannot receive him, because it isn't looking for him and doesn't recognize him. But you know him because he lives with you now and later will be in you."

INSIGHT

When we come to faith in Jesus the Messiah, that is a truly great gift in and of itself. In addition to this however, God knows that we need the added touch of true power, comfort and guidance. The Holy spirit is He who enables us to hear the Father's voice. He speaks to the Father on our behalf, when our human words fall short. He is the one who brings us peace when our world seems to have none. The same POWER that raised Jesus from the dead, is the same Power that gives us the ability to walk victoriously in a world that is not our own. Jesus promised the Holy Spirit as our Advocate, who would dwell in us and guide us.

REFLECTION

How does knowing the Holy Spirit is ALWAYS with you bring comfort and confidence?

____

____

____

____

____

____

APPLICATION

Write a prayer inviting the Holy Spirit to guide you into a specific area of your life today.

____

____

____

Day 2: The Power of the Holy Spirit

Date: _________________

Acts 1:8: "But you will receive power when the Holy Spirit comes upon you. And you will be my witnesses, telling people about me everywhere - in Jerusalem, throughout Judea, in Samaria, and to the ends of the earth."

INSIGHT

The Gospels tell us that our mandate is to go into all the world, share the Gospel story, and then help others to become followers of Jesus. We do this not only by sharing the Bible through preaching, teaching, and telling others HIS story, but also by sharing our story. But have you ever felt like your story and what Jesus has done in your life wouldn't really mean much to someone else? Without the Power of the Holy Spirit that dwells within us, that would perhaps be true. But something miraculous happens when we allow Him to work through and sometimes in spite of our personal testimonies. Ordinary words, from ordinary people become transformational in the lives of others. It is Holy Spirit that empowers believers to be witnesses for Christ, starting with our neighbor and extending far beyond.

REFLECTION

What does it mean to you to be a witness for Christ?

____

____

____

____

____

APPLICATION

Share an act of kindness or encouragement with someone today as a reflection of the Holy Spirit's power in your life. Share what you did.

____

____

Day 3: The Indwelling of the Spirit

Date: _________________

Romans 8:11: "The Spirit of God, who raised Jesus from the dead, lives in you. And just as God raised Christ Jesus from the dead, he will give life to your mortal bodies by this same Spirit living within

INSIGHT

In the New Testament the Holy Spirit is referred to as our *paracletos* in the Greek, which means "one who is called to one's side or aid." In much the same way, as an Ezer in the Old Testament, the Holy Spirit living in us enables us to do things that we cannot do by ourselves alone. The same Spirit who raised Jesus from the dead lives in you, giving life and strength.

REFLECTION

How does this truth encourage you in facing life's challenges?

____

____

____

____

____

____

APPLICATION

Reflect on one challenge you're facing and surrender it to God, trusting the Holy Spirit's power to sustain you.

____

____

____

____

Day 4: The Spirit of Truth

Date: ___________________

John 16:13: "When the Spirit of truth comes, he will guide you into all truth. He will not speak on his own but will tell you what he has heard. He will tell you about the future."

INSIGHT

Have you ever read a passage in the Bible and felt like you just didn't or couldn't understand it's meaning? It happens to me quite often. Maybe you read the same passage another day and then suddenly you feel connected to what is being said. That is the work of Holy Spirit in us. He is the power that enables our finite minds to connect and understand an infinite God. The Holy Spirit guides us into ALL truth, telling us what He hears directly from the Father, and helps us understand God's will for our lives.

REFLECTION

Are you seeking the Holy Spirit's guidance in your decisions? If not, start now and write them down here.

____

____

____

____

____

____

____

APPLICATION

Spend time in quiet reflection, asking the Holy Spirit to guide you in an area where you need clarity. Write down what He says to you.

____

____

____

Day 5: The Spirit's Role in Prayer

Date: _______________________

Romans 8:26-27: "And the Holy Spirit helps us in our weakness. For example, we don't know what God wants us to pray for. But the Holy Spirit prays for us with groanings that cannot be expressed in words. And the Father who knows all hearts knows what the Spirit is saying, for the Spirit pleads for us believers in harmony with God's own will."

INSIGHT

When my first husband passed away, our world was turned upside down. With two small children, no sure income, grieving our loss, and no place to call home, there were weeks and even months that I just had no words to express our needs to God. It is during these times that I just had to cling onto and trust in the words above. I just had to trust that Holy Spirit was pleading for us and leading us into God's own will for my little tribe of three. Today I can say that in those thirteen years, God has been faithful to guide and provide for us every step of the way. The Holy Spirit helps us in our weakness, interceding for us when we don't know what or how to pray. This is an example of His truth backed by personal experience, transforming not only my life, but hopefully the lives of others.

REFLECTION

How does Holy Spirit's intercession for us encourage you in times of struggle or uncertainty?

____

____

____

____

____

____

APPLICATION

Take time to pray today, allowing the Holy Spirit to guide your words and heart.

____

Day 6: The Holy Spirit as Comforter

Date: _________________

2 Corinthians 1:3-4: "All praise to God the Father of our Lord Jesus Christ. God is our merciful Father and the source of all comfort. He comforts us in all our troubles so that we can comfort others. When they are troubled, we will be able to give them the same comfort God has given us."

INSIGHT

Have you ever asked God, why He allowed this or that to happen in your life? Why did my daddy die when I was so young? Why did He allow me to become a widow at such a young age? Why did God allow me to be sexually assaulted by someone that I should have been able to trust? Why did my car fall into an irreparable state, when God knows it is my only means of transportation and supporting my family? All these questions are personal to my family and me, and I am certain that you have similar questions of your own. But think about it, how can Holy Spirit comfort us unless we go through things for which we need to be comforted? The Holy Spirit comforts us in our troubles SO THAT we can comfort others in their time of need. I have seen this for myself countless times with my own questions. I have shared my experiences with others going through similar circumstances and shared how God transformed my messes into His miracles. So, as you ask your "whys", trust that one day your experiences will comfort another brother or sister in need.

REFLECTION

How have you experienced the Holy Spirit's comfort in your life?

____

____

____

____

____

____

____

APPLICATION

Reach out to someone who may need encouragement today and offer them comfort or prayer. Remember it here.

148

Date: _________________

REFLECTION

Reflect on how the Holy Spirit has worked in your life this week.

____

____

____

____

____

____

PRAYER

Write a prayer thanking God for the gift of the Holy Spirit and asking Him to help you walk daily in His power.

____

____

____

____

____

____

APPLICATION

Write down one way you will intentionally rely on the Holy Spirit this week.

____

____

Week 2: The Fruit of the Spirit

To discover where we should be headed, by understanding how the Holy Spirit produces Christlike character in us. Living with love, joy, peace, patience, kindness, goodness, faithfulness, gentleness, and self-control.

Day 1: The Fruit of Love

Date: _________________

Galatians 5:22-23: "But the Holy Spirit produces this kind of fruit in our lives; love, joy, peace, patience, kindness, goodness, faithfulness, gentleness, and self-control. There is no law against these things."

1 Corinthians 13:4-7: "Love is patient and kind. Love is not jealous or boastful or proud or rude. It does not demand its own way. It is not irritable and keeps no record of being wronged. It does not rejoice about injustice but rejoices whenever the truth wins out. Love never gives up, never loses faith, is always hopeful, and endures through every circumstance.

INSIGHT

The first fruit of the Spirit is love, God's love, which is patient, kind, and unconditional. This love empowers us to love others as Christ loves us. This love is not something that we can generate on our own. In fact, 1 John 4:7 teaches us that LOVE is from GOD. When we find ourselves struggling to love others, we are most likely trying to do so in our own strength. So, when you feel that struggle, as we all do, stop and ask Holy Spirit to give you God's love. He is faithful and HE WILL DO IT!

REFLECTION

In what ways do you experience God's love, and how can you extend that love to others today?

____

____

____

____

____

____

APPLICATION

Identify someone in your life who could use a tangible expression of God's love. Send them a message or take them out for coffee to show your care. Make a record here of what you did with them.

Day 2: The Fruit of Joy

Date: _______________________

Romans 15:13: "I pray that God, the source of all hope, will find you completely with joy and peace because you trust in him. Then you will overflow with confident hope, through the power of the Holy Spirit."

Philippians 4:4: "Always be full of joy in the Lord. I say it again, REJOICE!"

INSIGHT

Joy is a fruit of the Spirit that comes from trusting in God's promises and His sovereignty. It's not dependent on circumstances, but on our relationship with Him. There is a popular expression: "Choose JOY." Although it may sound trite or cliche, there will be times where we will have to CHOOSE to partake of this fruit amid difficult circumstances.

REFLECTION

What areas in your life are you struggling to experience joy? How can you invite the Holy Spirit to fill you with joy despite your circumstances?

____

____

____

____

____

____

APPLICATION

Spend a few minutes today meditating on a Bible verse that reminds you of God's goodness. Let His promises stir joy in your heart.

____

____

Day 3: The Fruit of Peace

Date: _____________________

John 14:27: "I am leaving you with a gift - peace of mind and heart. And the peace that I give is a gift that the world cannot give. So, don't be troubled or afraid."

Philippians 4:6-7: "Don't worry about anything; instead, pray about everything. Tell God what you need and thank him for all he has done. Then you will experience God's peace, which exceeds anything we can understand. His peace will guard your hearts and minds as you live in Christ Jesus."

INSIGHT

So many times, we look for peace in all the wrong places: relationships, careers, governments, or hobbies. Although we may find some facsimile of peace in these worldly places, we WILL find that this peace is only temporary. And let's be real, the world you and I currently live in, displays anything but peace and tranquility. Lasting peace comes from KNOWING that God is in control. It comes from relinquishing control of our circumstances to Him. When we do this, God's peace will guard our hearts and minds in the midst of the chaos around us.

REFLECTION

Are there areas of anxiety or unrest in your life right now? How can you invite the Holy Spirit to bring peace into those situations?

____

____

____

____

____

____

APPLICATION

Write down a prayer of surrender for any area of your life where you're feeling anxious or unsettled. Ask the Holy Spirit to fill you with His peace.

____

158

Day 4: The Fruit of Patience

Date: _________________

James 5:7-8: "Dear brothers and sisters, be patient as you wait for the Lord's return. Consider the farmers who patiently wait for the rains in the fall and in the spring. They eagerly look for the valuable harvest to ripen. You too must be patient. Take courage for the coming of the Lord is near."

Romans 12:12: "Rejoice in our confident hope. Be patient in trouble and keep on praying."

INSIGHT

Does anyone besides me have issues with being patient? I think it is hard for me because patience requires waiting, and sometimes LOTS of it. We live in the age of instant everything. Everything from food to news comes to us at lightning speed. The world wide web, social media, and even the microwave in our kitchens, have conditioned us to getting what we want when we want it. The problem with this however, is that TIME itself belongs to God. The very concept of time is His doing. And the truth is waiting is just hard. Patience is a fruit of the Spirit that teaches us to wait on God's timing and remain steadfast in the face of trials.

REFLECTION

How have you seen God work in your life when you've had to wait? What areas do you need more patience in right now?

____

____

____

____

____

____

APPLICATION

Reflect on a current situation where you are being called to practice patience. Spend time in prayer, asking God to help you trust in His perfect timing.

____

____

Date: _________________

Ephesians 4:32: "Instead, be kind to each other, tenderhearted, forgiving one another, just as God through Christ has forgiven you."

Galatians 6:9-10: "So let's not get tired of doing what is good. At just the right time we will reap a harvest of blessing if we don't give up. Therefore, whenever we have the opportunity, we should do good to everyone - especially to those in the family of faith."

INSIGHT

Clearly, neither the Ephesians nor the Galatians lived in a kind or good environment. Does this sound familiar? It should. Our world today clearly is no different than theirs. Like them, we live in a fallen and broken world. Scripture tells us that NONE OF US is good. Therefore, none of us is kind on our own. We need a Helper, the Holy Spirit. Kindness and goodness go hand in hand; both are expressions of God's love, reflected in how we treat others.

REFLECTION

How do kindness and goodness manifest in your life? In what ways can you show God's goodness to those around you?

____

____

____

____

____

____

APPLICATION

Look for an opportunity today to perform an act of kindness, whether big or small. Let it be a reflection of God's love for others. "Remember what the Lord had you do to demonstrate His kindness."

Day 6: The Fruit of Faithfulness

Date: _______________________

Matthew 25:21: "The master was full of praise. 'Well done my good and faithful servant. You have been faithful in handling this small amount, so now I will give you many more responsibilities. Let's celebrate together.'"

1 Corinthians 4:2: "Now, a person who is put in charge as a manager, must be faithful."

INSIGHT

Do you tend to procrastinate? There is some small something that you need to do, but you voluntarily put it off even though you recognize that doing so could have an adverse outcome. I believe we all go through times when we do this. When we procrastinate, what we are really dealing with is a lack of this fruit of the Spirit. Faithfulness in the small things reveals our heart for God's kingdom. Faithfulness is never about big accomplishments but about consistent, daily obedience. So, do the little things and you will soon graduate to greater things.

REFLECTION

How does God view your faithfulness in the little things? How can you grow in your faithfulness to Him today?

____

____

____

____

____

____

APPLICATION

Ask God to help you be faithful in one area of your life where you've been neglecting your commitments. Take a step of obedience and record it here:

____

Day 7: The Fruit of Gentleness and Self-Control

Date: _______________

1 Peter 3:15-16: "Instead, you must worship Christ as Lord of your life. And if some-one asks you about your hope as a believer, always be ready to explain it. But do this in a gentle and respectful way. Keep your conscience clear. Then, if people speak against you, they will be ashamed when they see what a good life you live because you belong to Christ."

INSIGHT

Have you ever been in a situation where someone was trying to bring a word of correction, or just shared some bit of truth, but they did so in anything but a gentle or respectful way? How did you react? I must admit, I sometimes react badly. God is still and patiently working with me in this area. So, what is happening here? One person in this scenario is not exercising gentleness, and the other is not exercising self-control. Gentleness and self-control are vital for living out the Gospel. They are also vital for harmonious interpersonal relationships. These fruits, and in fact all the ones we have looked at this week, require practice and choice. Gentleness reflects humility and care, while self-control empowers us to resist temptation and live with one another in a Godly manner.

REFLECTION

How do you practice gentleness in your words and actions? Where do you struggle with self-control?

____

____

____

____

____

____

APPLICATION

Take a moment to reflect on how you can embody gentleness today, whether in how you speak to others or how you approach a situation. Pray for self-control in areas of weakness.

____

____

____

____

____

____

REFLECTION

This week, reflect on the fruit of the Spirit and how each one has been active in your life. In which area do you need the Holy Spirit to work in you most?

____

____

____

____

____

PRAYER

Write a prayer thanking God for the fruit of the Spirit and asking Him to cultivate them in your life. Pray for the Holy Spirit's help in growing in love, joy, peace, patience, kindness, goodness, faithfulness, gentleness, and self-control.

____

____

____

____

____

____

APPLICATION

Identify one fruit of the Spirit you want to focus on this week. Write down a specific action or attitude where you will actively pursue growth in that fruit.

Week 3: The Holy Spirit and Empowerment for Kingdom Work

To understand how the Holy Spirit EMPOWERS us to walk in purpose, EQUIP us for ministry, and CONTRIBUTE to the building of God's KINGDOM.

Day 1: The Holy Spirit Equips Us for Service

Date: _________________

1 Corinthians 12: 4-11: "There are different kinds of spiritual gifts, but the same spirit is the source of them all. There are different kinds of service, but we serve the same Lord. God works in different kinds of service, but we serve the same Lord. God works in different ways, but it is the same God who does the work in all of us. A spiritual gift is given to each of us so we can help each other. To one person the Spirit gives the ability to give wise advice; to another the same Spirit gives a message of special knowledge. The same Spirit gives great faith to another, and to someone else the one Spirit gives the gift of healing. He gives one person the power to perform miracles, and another the ability to prophesy. He gives someone else the ability to discern whether a message is from the Spirit of God, or from another spirit. Still another person is given the ability to speak in unknown languages, while another is given the ability to interpret what is being said. It is the one and only Spirit who distributes these gifts. He alone decides which gift each person should have."

INSIGHT

The Bible tells us not to grow weary in doing good (Galatians 6:9). I believe that in order to accomplish this, we must be connected to an infinite source. The Holy Spirit distributes spiritual gifts to believers for the purpose of building up the body of Christ. These gifts EMPOWER us to serve others and ADVANCE God's kingdom.

REFLECTION

How have you seen the Holy Spirit's gifts active in your life? How are you currently using your gifts to serve others?

____

____

____

____

____

____

APPLICATION

Take time to reflect on the gifts you have been given and identify one area where you can intentionally use your gift to serve someone else.

____

____

____

____

____

____

Date: _____________________

Acts 4:29-31: "'And now, O Lord, hear their threats, and give us, your servants, great boldness in preaching your word. Stretch out your hand with healing power; many miraculous signs and wonders be done through the name of your Holy servant Jesus.' After this prayer, the meeting place shook, and they were filled with the Holy Spirit. Then they preached the word of God with boldness."

INSIGHT

We have all been there… that moment of internal conflict. Someone comes across our path who is struggling for direction, understanding, or lasting truth. We know that we have the answer, Jesus. But we wonder if we should share that truth, or if what we have to share will be received. We ask ourselves; "What will this person think of me?" Out of our own fears, we lack the boldness to share the eternal truth that we possess. After receiving the Holy Spirit, the disciples were EMPOWERED to speak the word of God BOLDLY. The Spirit gives us courage to live out our faith without fear of the world's opposition.

REFLECTION

Where in your life do you need the boldness of the Holy Spirit to speak or act in faith?

____

____

____

____

____

____

APPLICATION

Write down an area of your life where you want to be bolder in your faith. Ask the Holy Spirit to fill you with courage to step out in obedience.

____

____

Day 3: The Holy Spirit Leads Us in Prayer

Date: _______________________

Romans 8:26-27: "And the Holy Spirit helps us in our weakness. For example, we don't know what God wants us to pray for. But the Holy Spirit prays for us with groanings that cannot be expressed in words, And the Father who knows all hearts know what the Spirit is saying, for the Spirit pleads for us believers in harmony with God's own will."

INSIGHT

Have you ever wanted to pray for someone, a friend, a coworker, a family member, or even yourself, but felt like your words fell short? What do you do in that moment? Just like me, you are encountering your human weakness. We could just walk away right? But there is an alternative. It is as simple as asking the Holy Spirit for help. He helps us in our weakness, especially through prayer. He speaks to the Father for us when we don't know how to pray and guides us in aligning our hearts with God's will.

REFLECTION

How have you experienced the Holy Spirit's help in your prayer life?

____

____

____

____

____

____

APPLICATION

Spend time in quiet prayer, inviting the Holy Spirit to guide your words. Write a prayer asking Him to help you align your desires with God's will.

____

____

____

____

Day 4: The Holy Spirit Brings Transformation

Date: _________________

2 Corinthians 3:18: "So all of us who have had that veil removed can see and reflect the glory of the Lord. And the Lord - who is the Spirit - makes us more and more like him as we are changed into his glorious image."

INSIGHT

I love butterflies! Their delicate strength is a thing of true beauty. But they were not always so and in fact they couldn't even fly. Once they were caterpillars. When a caterpillar goes into its cocoon, it goes through a death and a resurrection process. Its body is completely consumed, molecules rearranged, until it emerges as a completely different thing than it was before. But even butterflies are not beautiful when they first emerge from that cocoon. It takes time for their wings to expand so that they can fly. Caterpillars always have the potential to be something more than they are and so do we. When we come to know Jesus, we clearly don't look, think, or act much like him. It takes time for the old man to die so that the new man can reach the potential that God intended. It is a daily process of dying to the old and embracing the new and even this is not in our own strength. The Holy Spirit transforms us into the image of Christ. As we surrender to Him, He continually works in our hearts to shape us more into God's likeness.

REFLECTION

What areas of your life need transformation by the Holy Spirit?

____

____

____

____

____

APPLICATION

Write down one area where you long to see transformation and surrender it to the Holy Spirit. Ask Him to work in you, making you more like Christ.

Day 5: The Holy Spirit and Our Identity in Christ

Date: _______________

Romans 8:14-17: "For all who are led by the Spirit of God are the children of God. So, you have not received a spirit that makes you fearful slaves. Instead, you received God's Spirit when he adopted you as his own children. Now we call him 'Abba Father.' For his spirit joins with our spirit to affirm that we are God's children. And since we are his children, we are his heirs. In fact, together with Christ we are heirs of God's Glory. But if we are to share his glory, we must also share his suffering."

INSIGHT

For many of us, perhaps most of us in fact, the idea of a loving and accepting father is hard to identify with. Maybe we never knew our earthly father. Maybe he died when we were young, as is me and my children's case. Maybe we came from a divorced family. Or maybe he was always in our homes, but was emotionally distant, overly demanding, or even abusive. In a way, we feel enslaved to what we experienced with our earthly fathers and struggle to receive the unconditional kind of love that God, our heavenly Father, offers us. In this scripture however, it is clear that the Holy Spirit confirms our identity as children of God, giving us the assurance that we are LOVED and ACCEPTED by the Father.

REFLECTION

How does the Holy Spirit confirm your identity as a beloved daughter of God?

____

____

____

____

____

____

____

APPLICATION

Reflect on your identity in Christ and write a declaration of who you are in Him. Use Scripture to remind yourself of your worth and who you truly are in Christ Jesus.

Day 6: The Holy Spirit Enables Us to Love Others

Date: _________________

Romans 5:5: "And this hope will not lead to disappointment. For we know how dearly God loves us, because he has given us the Holy Spirit, to fill our hearts with his love."

INSIGHT

Have you heard the expression, "you can't give what you never had?" While in the natural this is true, the playing field changes when we come into relationship with Jesus. True love can only come from God. The Bible says the Holy Spirit pours God's love into our hearts, enabling us to love others with the same love that Christ has shown us.

REFLECTION

How does the Holy Spirit help you love others, especially when it's difficult?

____

____

____

____

____

____

APPLICATION

Identify one person or situation where you need God's love to flow through you. Write a prayer asking the Holy Spirit to empower you to love others as Christ loves you.

____

____

____

____

____

Date: _____________________

REFLECTION

Reflect on how the Holy Spirit has empowered you in various areas of your life this week. In what ways have you seen His work in equipping you, leading you, and transforming you?

____

____

____

____

____

____

PRAYER

Write a prayer thanking God for the empowering work of the Holy Spirit in your life. Ask Him to continue equipping you for His kingdom work and to help you walk in His power and purpose.

____

____

____

____

____

APPLICATION

Identify one action or change you want to make this week that reflects your willingness to step into the empowerment of the Holy Spirit.

____

____

____

Week 4: Living Out the Power of the Holy Spirit in Community

To begin to walk out our faith in community by grasping how the Holy Spirit ENABLES us to live out our faith within the body of Christ, EMPOWERING us to build a supportive, loving community. The Holy Spirit equips us not only for individual transformation but also, for contributing to the unity and strength of the church.

Day 1: The Importance of Community

Date: _________________

Hebrews 10:24-25: "Let us think of ways to motivate on another to acts of love and good works. And let us not neglect our meeting together, as some people do, but encourage one another, especially now that the day of his return is drawing near."

INSIGHT

The Bible emphasizes the importance of gathering with fellow believers, encouraging one another and spurring one another on toward love and good works. After COVID and the lock down, I really struggled with getting back to church. I knew that I needed the fellowship of other believers. I was the midst of a severe bout of depression, and I remember my counselor telling me that I was needed and thinking to myself, "What could I possibly have to offer anyone?" Have you ever felt this way? This speaks to the very heart of becoming and being an Ezer. We all have our own unique stories and life experiences. The true beauty is that if we allow Holy Spirit to use us as Ezers, our stories and life experiences make us each uniquely qualified to help others in a way that they cannot help themselves. God never wastes anything. The Holy Spirit enables us to live in community with others, sharing burdens and celebrating joys.

REFLECTION

How have you been encouraged by the community of believers in your life?

____

____

____

____

____

____

APPLICATION

Reach out to someone in your church or community today to encourage them. Write them a note or send a text to express your love and support. What did you do?

____

Day 2: The Holy Spirit and Unity in the Body of Christ

Date: _______________________

1 Corinthians 12:12-13: "The human body has many parts, but the many parts make up one whole body. So, it is with the body of Christ. Some of us are Jews, some are Gentiles, some are slaves, and some are free. But we have all been baptized into one body by one Spirit and we all share the same Spirit."

INSIGHT

Okay ladies, have you ever had a hang nail? They can be really painful right? And that one little wound on the end of your finger can make using that hand effectively more difficult than it needs to or was ever intended to be. Point being, the Church is not effective when one of its parts, you or me, is missing. The Holy Spirit unites believers in Christ, forming one body. We each have different roles and gifts, but we are all one in the Spirit, working together for the common good.

REFLECTION

How do you experience unity in your church or community? How can you contribute to unity in the body of Christ?

____

____

____

____

____

____

____

APPLICATION

Identify one area where you can contribute to fostering unity in your community: whether through serving, listening, or supporting.

____

____

____

Date: _______________________

1 Corinthians 12:4-11"There are different kinds of spiritual gifts, but the same Spirit is the source of them all. There are different kinds of service, but we serve the same Lord, God works in different ways, but it is the same God who does the work in all of us. A spiritual gift is given to each of us so we can help each other. To one person the Spirit gives the ability to give wise advice; to another the Spirit gives a message of special knowledge. The same Spirit gives great faith to another, and to someone else the one Spirit gives the gift of healing. He gives one person the power to perform miracles, and another the ability to prophesy. He gives someone else the ability to discern whether a message is from the Spirit of God or from another spirit. Still another person is given the ability to speak in unknown languages, while another is given the ability to inter-pret what is being said. It is the one and only Spirit who distributes all these gifts. He alone decides which gift each person should have."

Romans 12:6-8: "In his grace, God has given us different gifts for doing things well. So, if God has given you the ability to prophesy, speak out with as much faith as God has given you. If your gift is serving others, serve them well. If you are a teacher, teach well. If your gift is to encourage others, be encouraging. If it is giving, give generously. If God has given you leadership ability, take the responsibility seriously. And if you have a gift for showing kindness to others, do it gladly."

INSIGHT

The Holy Spirit gives spiritual gifts to each believer. We cannot and MUST NOT try to "manufac-ture" them. When we do, we are only benefiting ourselves and our gifts are meant to be used for the edification of the church and are of His choosing. Our gifts are not for personal gain but for the benefit of the body of Christ.

REFLECTION

What spiritual gifts has the Holy Spirit given you? How have you used them to serve the church?

____

____

____

____

____

____

____

APPLICATION

Take time to reflect on your spiritual gifts. Prayerfully consider how you can use your gifts in service to others this week.

____

____

____

____

____

____

____

Day 4: The Fruit of the Spirit in Community

Date: _______________________

Galatians 5:22-23: "But the Holy Spirit produces this kind of fruit in our lives; love joy, peace, patience, kindness, goodness, faithfulness, gentleness, and self-control. There is no law against these things."

Ephesians 4:1-3: "Therefore I, a prisoner for serving the Lord, beg you to lead a life worthy of your calling, for you have been called by God. Always be humble and gentle. Be patient with each other, making allowance for each other's faults because of your love. Make every effort to keep yourselves united in the Spirit, binding yourselves together with peace."

INSIGHT

The fruits of the Spirit are not only meant to grow within us, but are also to be expressed in our relationships with others. As we cultivate love, joy, peace, patience, kindness, and other fruits, we contribute to the health and vibrancy of the Christian community.

REFLECTION

Which fruit of the Spirit do you feel called to cultivate more in your interactions with others?

____

____

____

____

____

____

APPLICATION

Consider a relationship in your life where you can practice one of the fruits of the Spirit today. Let the Holy Spirit empower you to bring peace, joy, or patience into that relationship. Who would this person be and how do you believe the Holy Spirit would have you walk forward with what He tells you?

Day 5: The Holy Spirit and Conflict Resolution

Date: _______________________

Matthew 18:15-17: "If another believer sins against you, go privately and point out the offense. If the other person listens and confesses it, you have won that person back. But if you are unsuccessful, take one or two others with you and go back again, so that everything you say may be confirmed by two or three witnesses. If the person still refuses to listen, take your case to the church. Then if he or she won't accept the church's decision, treat that person as a pagan or a corrupt tax collector.

" Romans 12:18: "Do all that you can to live in peace with everyone."

INSIGHT

Scripture gives us clear counsel on how to resolve conflicts. And although it is not always, like never, comfortable, the Holy Spirit equips us to navigate conflict in healthy ways. This requires great humility and discipline, because our fallen and natural tendency is one of 'tit for tat'. We are called to seek RECONCILIATION with others, PURSUING peace and unity in the body of Christ.

REFLECTION

Have you experienced conflict in your relationships recently? How can the Holy Spirit help you approach this situation with love and truth?

____

____

____

____

____

____

APPLICATION

If you are currently experiencing conflict, take a step toward a resolution today. Write a prayer asking the Holy Spirit to give you wisdom, humility, and grace in approaching reconciliation.

Day 6: The Holy Spirit as a Comforter in Community

Date: _______________________

John 14:16: "And I will ask the Father, and he will give you another Advocate, who will never leave you."

2 Corinthians 1:3-4: "All praise to God, the Father of our Lord Jesus Christ. God is our merciful Father and the source of all comfort; He comforts in all our troubles so that we can comfort others. When they are troubled, we will be able to give them the same comfort God has given us."

INSIGHT

The Holy Spirit not only empowers us but also brings comfort and encouragement in times of hardship. This again reflects part of becoming an Ezer. Our being comforted means that we went through some sort of difficulty for which we needed the comfort of the Holy Spirit. Remember earlier in the week I said that God doesn't waste anything? But we can waste the comfort He has given to us. Comfort is a blessing, and as Christians, God blesses not so that we can just keep it to ourselves, but so that we in turn can bless those around us.

REFLECTION

How have you experienced the Holy Spirit's comfort in your life? How can you be a source of comfort to someone else today?

____

____

____

____

____

____

APPLICATION

Reach out to someone who may be grieving, struggling, or going through a difficult time. Offer them words of comfort or simply listen with empathy. Record here what you did and with whom?

7: Reflection and Prayer: Walking in the Power of the Holy Spirit

Date: ___________________

REFLECTION

Reflect on the ways the Holy Spirit has worked in your community and relationships over the past week. How has He empowered you to contribute to the unity and health of the body of Christ?

____

____

____

____

____

____

PRAYER

Write a prayer thanking God for the gift of community and asking the Holy Spirit to continue to work in you and through you to build up the body of Christ. Identify one way you can continue to invest in the community and contribute to the spiritual health of others this week. Write down your commitment and ask God for strength to follow through.

____

____

____

____

____

____

Wrap-Up Week 13: Embracing the Fullness of God's Call

Bringing it all together

To simply reflect on our journey of SPIRITUAL GROWTH and EMPOWERMENT through the study of "Ezer," how we have learned to walk in the power of the Holy Spirit, nd how to continue moving forward in God's purpose for our lives.

Day 1: Reflecting on God's Love for Women

Date: _____________________

Jeremiah 31:3: "Long ago the Lord said to Israel: 'I have loved you, my people, with an everlasting love. With unfailing love, I have drawn you to myself'"

1 John 3:1: "See how very much our Father loves us, for he calls us his children, and that is what we are! But the people who belong to this world don't recognize that we are God's children because they don't know him."

INSIGHT

God's love for you is UNSHAKABLE and UNWAVERING. You are precious in His sight, and He has been with you through EVERY step of your journey. The more you UNDERSTAND the depth of God's love for you, the MORE you are EMPOWERED to live out your PURPOSE AS A WOMAN OF GOD!

REFLECTION

Looking back over this study, how have you experienced God's love in new or deeper ways?

____

____

____

____

____

____

APPLICATION

Take a moment to journal about how God's love has shaped your identity. Write a prayer of gratitude, thanking Him for His enduring love and asking Him to help you walk in the fullness of that love.

____

____

Date: ________________________

Luke 7:36-50: "One of the Pharisees asked Jesus to have dinner with him, so Jesus went to his home and sat down to eat. When a certain immoral woman from that city heard he was eating there, she brought a beautiful alabaster jar filled with expensive perfume. Then she knelt behind him at his feet, weeping. Her tears fell on his feet, and she wiped them off with her hair. Then she kept kissing his feet and putting perfume on them. When the Pharisee who had invited him saw this, Simon said to himself, 'If this man were a prophet, he would know what kind of woman is touching him. She's a sinner!' The Jesus answered his thoughts. 'Simon.' he said to the Pharisee, 'I have something to say to you.' 'Go ahead, Teacher,' Simon replied. Then Jesus told him this story: 'A man loaned money to two people - 500 pieces of silver, to one and 50 to the other. But neither of them could repay him, so he kindly forgave them both, canceling their debts. Who do you suppose loved him more after that?' Simon answered, 'I suppose the one for whom he cancelled the larger debt.' 'That's right,' Jesus said. Then he turned to the woman and said to Simon, 'Look at this woman kneeling here. When I entered your home, you didn't offer me water to wash the dust from my feet, but she has washed them with her tears and wiped them with her hair. You didn't greet me with a kiss, but from the time I first came in, she has not stopped kissing my feet. You neglected the courtesy of olive oil to anoint my head, but she has anointed my feet with rare perfume. I tell you, her sins - and they are many - have been forgiven, so she has shown me much love. But a person who is forgiven little shows only little love' Then Jesus said to the woman, 'Your sins are forgiven.' The men at the table said among themselves, 'Who is this man, that he goes around forgiving sins?' And Jesus said to the woman, 'Your faith has saved you; go in peace'"

John 4:1-26: "He had to go through Samaria on the way. Eventually he came to the Samaritan village of Sychar, near the field that Jacob gave his son Joseph. Jacob's well was there; and Jesus, tired from the long walk, sat wearily beside the well about noontime. Soon a Samaritan woman cane to draw water, and Jesus said to her, 'Please give me a drink.' He was alone at the time because his Disciples had gone into the village to buy some food. The woman was surprised, for Jews refuse to have anything to do with Samaritans. She said to Jesus, 'You are a Jew, and I am a Samaritan woman. Why are you asking me for a drink?' Jesus replied, 'If you only knew the gift God has for you, you would ask me, and I would give you living water.'" "But sir, you don't have a rope or a bucket,' she said, and this well is very deep. Where would you get this living water? And besides, do you think you're greater than our ancestor Jacob, who gave us this well? How can you offer better water than he and his sons and his animals enjoyed,' Jesus replied, "Anyone who drinks this water will soon become thirsty again. But those who drink the water I give will never be thirsty again. It becomes a fresh bubbling spring within them giving them eternal life.' 'Please, sir,' the woman said, 'give me this water! Then I'll never be thirsty again, and I won't have to come here to get water.' 'Go and get your husband.' Jesus told her. 'I don't have a husband,' the woman replied. Jesus said, 'You're right! You don't have a husband - for you have had five husbands, and you aren't even married to the man you're living with now. You certainly spoke the truth!' 'Sir,' the woman said, 'you must be a prophet. So, tell me, why is it you Jews insist that Jerusalem is the only place of worship, while we Samaritans claim it is here at Mount Gerazim, where our ancestors worshipped?' Jesus replied, 'Believe me, dear woman, the time is coming when it will no longer matter whether you worship the Father on this mountain or in Jerusalem. You Samaritans know very little about the one you worship, while we Jews know all about hum, for salvation comes through the Jews. But the time is coming - indeed it is here now - when true worshipers will worship the Father in spirit and in truth. The Father is looking for those who will worship him that way. For God is Spirit, so those who worship him must worship him in spirit and in truth.' The woman said, 'know the Messiah is coming - the one who is called Christ. When he comes, he will explain everything to us.' Then Jesus told her, 'I AM the MESSIAH!'"

INSIGHT

Jesus valued and elevated women in ways that defied the cultural norms of His time. Through His interactions with women, He demonstrated deep care, compassion, and respect. As a woman of God, you are not only VALUED by God but also called to LIVE IN THE FREEDOM OF YOUR IDENTITY IN CHRIST.

REFLECTION

How has your understanding of Christ's treatment of women impacted the way you view yourself and your purpose?

____

____

____

____

____

____

APPLICATION

Reflect on one woman in the Bible whose story has resonated with you over the past few weeks. Write about how her life has inspired your own walk with God.

____

____

Day 3: Empowerment Through the Holy Spirit

Date: _____________________

Acts 1:8: "But the believers who were scattered preached the Good News about Jesus wherever they went."

Romans 8:11: "The Spirit of God, who raised Jesus from the dead, lives in you. And just as God raised Christ Jesus from the dead, he will give life to your mortal bodies by the same Spirit living within you."

INSIGHT

The HOLY SPIRIT EMPOWERS YOU to live a life of PURPOSE, to walk in BOLDNESS, and to BE a LIGHT in the world. The HOLY SPIRIT EQUIPS YOU to LIVE out the calling that GOD has PLACED on your life.

REFLECTION

In what ways has the Holy Spirit empowered you during this study? How have you seen His power working in your life?

____

____

____

____

____

____

APPLICATION

Take a moment to journal about an area of your life where you desire to experience the power of the Holy Spirit in greater measure. Ask Him to fill you afresh and empower you for the journey ahead.

____

____

Day 4: The Role of Women in God's Kingdom

Date: _______________________

Esther 4:14: "If you keep quiet at a time like this, deliverance and relief for the Jews will arise from some other place, but you and your relatives will die. Who knows if perhaps you were made queen for just such a time as this?"

Romans 12:4-5: "Just as our bodies have many parts and each part has a special function, so it is with Christ's body. We are many parts of one body, and we all belong to each other."

INSIGHT

God has called women to be KEY PLAYERS in His kingdom. Just as He used Esther to save a nation, He has equipped you with gifts, talents, and a purpose to IMPACT THE WORLD AROUND YOU and beyond.

REFLECTION

What role do you feel God is calling you to play in His kingdom?

____

____

____

____

____

____

APPLICATION

Take time today to think about how you can live out your purpose in the world around you. Whether it's in your family, workplace, or community, ask God to reveal practical ways you can serve Him with the gifts He has given you.

____

____

____

Day 5: Walking BOLDLY in Your Identity in Christ

Date: _______________________

Galatians 2:20: "My old self has been crucified with Christ. It is no longer I who live, but Christ who lives in me. So, I live in this earthly body by trusting in the Son of God, who loved me and gave himself for me."

1 Peter 2:9: "But you are not like that, for you are a chosen people. You are royal priests, a holy nation, God's very own possession. As a result, you can show others the goodness of God, for he called you out of the darkness into his wonderful light."

INSIGHT

You are no longer DEFINED by the world's standards BUT BY YOUR IDENTITY IN CHRIST. Your TRUE WORTH and VALUE are FOUND IN HIM. As you embrace your identity, you can walk boldly in the call God has placed on your life.

REFLECTION

How has understanding your identity in Christ changed the way you view yourself and your purpose?

____

____

____

____

____

____

APPLICATION

Write a declaration of your identity in Christ. Speak it over your life daily and commit to walking confidently in who you are as a daughter of the King.

____

____

____

Day 6: Living Out the Fruits of the Spirit

Date: _______________________

Galatians 5:22-23: "But the Holy Spirit produces this kind of fruit in our lives; love, joy, peace, patience, kindness, goodness, faithfulness, gentleness, and self-control. There is no law against these things!"

Colossians 3:12-14: "Since God chose you to be the holy people he loves, you must clothe yourselves with tender-hearted mercy, kindness, humility, gentleness and patience. make allowances for each other's faults and forgive anyone who offends you. Remember, the lord forgave you, so you must forgive others. Above all, clothe yourselves with love, which binds us all together in perfect harmony."

INSIGHT

The fruits of the Spirit are not just personal characteristics, but reflections of God's work in and through you. As you continue to grow in your relationship with the Holy Spirit, you will see the fruits of the Spirit more fully manifest in your life.

REFLECTION

Which fruit of the Spirit has been most evident in your life throughout this study? Which fruit do you feel God is calling you to?

____

____

____

____

____

____

APPLICATION

Choose one fruit of the Spirit to focus on this week. Write a plan for how you will intentionally cultivate this fruit in your life and relationships.

____

Day 7: Final Reflection and Prayer

Date: _________________

REFLECTION

As you look back over the past 12 weeks, take time to reflect on how God has moved in your life. How have you grown in your understanding of His love for you? How has the Holy Spirit empowered you to walk in your purpose and calling?

____

____

____

____

____

____

PRAYER

Write a prayer of thanksgiving for the growth and transformation you've experienced during this study. Thank God for His constant love, His call on your life, and the empowerment of the Holy Spirit. Ask Him to continue guiding you as you walk in the fullness of your calling as an "Ezer".

____

____

____

____

____

____

APPLICATION

Choose one area of your life where you feel called to continue growing. Write down specific actions you will take to continue walking in the power of the Holy Spirit and fulfilling God's purpose for your life.

Closing Encouragement

You have now completed the "Ezer" study and have learned how to walk in the fullness of your identity as a woman of God.

EMBRACE the empowerment of the Holy Spirit

and continue to walk

CONFIDENTLY in your CALLING.

you are a BELOVED DAUGHTER of God,

UNIQUELY CREATED for HIS purposes.

Your journey DOESN'T END here - it CONTINUES

as you LIVE IT OUT,

sharing God's love with others,

and contributing to His kingdom.

Stay ROOTED in His love,

GROUNDED in His Word,

and EMPOWERED by His Spirit

as you step BOLDLY into the future

HE HAS PREPARED FOR YOU!

www.ingramcontent.com/pod-product-compliance
Lightning Source LLC
Chambersburg PA
CBHW081142130726
47996CB00009B/2950